15
WEALTH&
DREAM

15
WEALTH&
DREAM

窮理查年鑑
————精華珍藏版————

Poor Richard's Almanack

經典長銷
×
全新增訂

班傑明‧富蘭克林◎著
邱振訓◎譯

WEALTH& DREAM 15 **窮理查年鑑‧精華珍藏版**

原著書名	Poor Richard's Almanack
作　者	班傑明‧富蘭克林（Benjamin Franklin）
譯　者	邱振訓
美術編輯	吳佩真、李緹瀅
主　編	高煜婷
總編輯	林許文二

出　版	柿子文化事業有限公司
地　址	11677臺北市羅斯福路五段158號2樓
業務專線	（02）89314903#15
讀者專線	（02）89314903#9
傳　真	（02）29319207
郵撥帳號	19822651柿子文化事業有限公司
投稿信箱	editor@persimmonbooks.com.tw
服務信箱	service@persimmonbooks.com.tw

初版一刷	2011年09月
七刷	2011年10月
二版一刷	2016年04月
三版一刷	2022年10月
定　價	新臺幣320元
ISBN	978-986-5496-96-8

業務行政	鄭淑娟、陳顯中

～柿子在秋天火紅 文化在書中成熟～

國家圖書館出版品預行編目(CIP)資料

窮理查年鑑／班傑明‧富蘭克林（Benjamin Franklin）
著；邱振訓譯. -- 三版. -- 臺北市：柿子文化事業有限公司,
2022.10
精華珍藏版
　面； 公分. -- (Wealth&Dream；15)
譯自：Poor Richard's Almanack
ISBN 978-986-5496-96-8（平裝）

1.CST:格言

192.8　　　　　　　　　　　　　　　111012017

言辭可以顯示一個人的機智，
但行動才真正展現出他的意思。

關於富蘭克林的那些事……

富蘭克林是十八世紀著名的偉人，他的多才多藝及其對國家的卓越貢獻，讓他擁有如「現代文明之父」、「美國聖人」、「美國革命之父」等眾多稱號。雖然現在每張百元美鈔都印上富蘭克林的肖像，將他視為財富象徵、資本主義精神的最佳代表，但他勤奮、節儉的人格，才是他之所以成功，並成為美國民眾及商業成功人士效法對象的主要原因——鋼鐵大王卡內基、投資大師巴菲特、查理‧蒙格等人更將他視為心目中的英雄。

多才多藝的父親

源於英格蘭的富蘭克林家族，世代擁有十二公頃的自由領地，並以打鐵為副業，由每代長子繼承家業。班傑明‧富蘭克林的父親名叫約賽亞，與三哥班傑明的感情特別深厚。班傑明到倫敦學習染絲綢，約賽亞則跟在呢絨染匠的二哥約翰身邊當學徒。

約賽亞家族為虔誠的清教徒，為了擺脫非國教信徒所受到的宗教迫害，他在一六八二年帶著妻子及三個孩子遷居新英格蘭波士頓城，妻子又生了四個孩子後，便離開人世。約賽亞之後續娶了教師家族彼得‧福格爾之女——阿拜亞‧福格爾為繼室，阿拜亞又為他生了十個子女。

到了北美殖民地後，因染布業生意慘澹，約賽亞便改以製作肥皂、蠟燭維生。他多才多藝，除了繪畫，還時常拉提琴唱歌自娛；另外，他對公共事務的熱誠、處事公正且善於決斷，所以家中常有仕紳領袖登門拜訪，詢問他對小鎮的見解與意見，而他自己也時常擔任訴訟的仲裁者。

豐富的學徒生涯

一七〇六年一月十七日，班傑明·富蘭克林出生，約塞亞用摯愛兄長的名字為自己的兒子命名。富蘭克林是十七名子女中最小的兒子，下面還有兩個妹妹。在其他兒子在各種行業當學徒之時，由於約賽亞想將富蘭克林以「什一稅」奉獻給教會，便在八歲時送他進法語學校就讀，但礙於家庭經濟負擔過重，富蘭克林十歲時就輟學返家，幫助父親經營事業。

富蘭克林從小便喜歡航海，很小就學會游泳和划船，對肥皂、蠟燭業興趣缺缺。父親曾經帶他四處觀摩木匠、泥瓦匠、鏇工、銅匠鋪，也讓他跟哥哥班傑明的兒子薩穆爾學過製刀，這些豐富經驗讓富蘭克林對各種機械都略知一二，也能在家中做些簡單的機械實驗。最後，富蘭克林選擇到哥哥詹姆士的印刷廠當學徒。

喜愛閱讀的富蘭克林輟學後仍抓緊時間自學，得到的零用錢都花在買書上；也因從事印刷業認識了書店學徒和幾個藏書愛好者，他常在晚間向人借書，熬夜閱讀後趕在第二天一早送還，並悉心留意書的清潔，從不汙損。這段時間，富蘭克林的閱讀日益艱深專業，從哲學、數學、邏輯到修辭學，同時一邊練習寫作，並在閱讀特萊昂的書後，成為一個素食者（但沒有很嚴格）。詹姆士於一七二一年八月辦了自己的報紙《新英格蘭報》，富蘭克林便藉機偷偷以化名「賽倫斯·杜古德」的女子身分，用第一人稱寫稿投稿。

後來，富蘭克林因與其兄詹姆士不合，而在十七歲時偷偷離家到紐約，輾轉到費城、英國倫敦繼續從事印刷業。不論在何處，他都不斷對公共事務發表評論、對政府投書、發表各式文章，並且也獲得各階層的熱烈迴響與高銷售量，因而認識許多名人並得到青睞，最終得以獨立開辦自己的印刷所，還以勤謹商人的形象深植人心。辦報、雜誌、出版作家作品、開設文具店……甚至紐約、北卡羅來納、喬治亞、費城附近的蘭卡斯特都有他的合夥人。

風靡歐美的 《窮理查年鑑》

一七三二年，富蘭克林不僅創辦了美洲第一所圖書館，發行了他獨資經營出版印刷業以後的第一份報紙，還開始出版他風行一時的曆書。當時，每個家庭都有一本曆書，可說是發行最廣泛的出版物；它的體積剛好可以放進口袋，人們能從中查到月亮圓缺、潮汐漲落、季節變換；還記錄食譜、笑話、詩歌、諺語和各種奇聞怪事；每頁日曆的空白處，可以用來寫日記；孩子也能利用曆書識字。

一部暢銷曆書不僅能為出版者帶來巨大財富，還能使編者的聲名遠播。在別家競爭者的曆書早已上市一個多月之際，富蘭克林十二月十九日才開始發行一七三三年的《窮理查年鑑》，但僅三個星期，他的曆書就再刷了三次，發行量大大超越其他曆書。

曆書書名的「窮理查」據說是從哥哥詹姆士所發行的《窮羅賓曆書》而來，而《窮理查年鑑》第一年中關於泰坦·利茲將死於一七三三年十月的預言，可能是學習二十五年前倫敦的喬納森·斯威夫特對約翰·帕特里奇的惡作劇。不過，「窮理查」對人生的體悟及反諷的幽默，全是富蘭克林所原創。

連續二十五年編纂《窮理查年鑑》，富蘭克林的用意在於「教育」。將成語、格言印在書中頁面的空白處，目的就在於教導大眾學習各種美德，以勤儉創造財富。

《窮理查年鑑》不只風行美洲，還席捲了歐洲，不僅為富蘭克林帶來財富，也讓他得到好聲譽。後來，富蘭克林把這些智慧的言語集中編輯，當作智者亞伯拉罕在拍賣場上的演講，名為〈財富之路〉，放在一七五八年《窮理查年鑑》卷首。這些雋語讓讀者印象深刻，而且相當受到歡迎；隨著時光流逝，儘管《窮理查年鑑》原本早已散佚，〈財富之路〉卻以精華版的方式，一再地被引用和閱讀。

多重身分，眼光獨到，投資、教育、研究一把罩

富蘭克林的家設備完善，除了書房、實驗室之外，連印刷所、店鋪、帳房以及一七三七年接管的郵局都設在家中——他幾乎不用出門，就能從事所有活動。他販售的貨品也愈來愈多，從文具、書籍、食品，到廚房用具，超過五十餘種；他甚至還為造紙商人收購破布呢！他精通法文、拉丁文、西班牙文、義大利文，一邊思考、研究、寫作，一邊處理、應付商務、公眾及家庭的各類事務，愈來愈繁忙，也愈來愈富有。

富蘭克林是有名的科學家與發明家，不管是電學、大氣變化、氣流學、龍捲風、洋流，都有深入研究，而最為人所知的發明物則是避雷針。與兒子威廉在大雷雨中用風箏吸引雷電的實驗最為人津津樂道，並創造我們今天還在使用的正電、負電、放電等專有名詞。其他發明還有蛙鞋、可省四分之三燃料的節能暖爐、讓近視眼與老花眼者同時可看近看遠的雙焦距眼鏡。他同時也是一位數學家，八階與十六階的魔術方陣都難不倒他，而身為音樂家的他，更發明了玻璃琴。

身為一位教育家，他每週與好友聚會一次，發表對政治、哲學、道德的意見，為整個國家社會把脈；北美第一個公共圖書館制度也出自他之手，讓北美其他地區皆紛紛倣效；之後他創辦賓州大學，讓教育更加落實於社會大眾。

貢獻卓著的政治生涯

每年富蘭克林都從其他合夥人、城內房地產和貸款利息獲得許多財富，在有錢有閒之餘，也研究哲學、科學，然而，他更重視社會公益，在報章雜誌中不時刊載他的改革理念，也深獲大眾愛戴。政府各部門幾乎同時邀他效勞——市議會議員、治安推事、市參議員、州議會議員……，在政治上，充分發揮其影響力，也朝理想步

步邁進。不論參與《巴黎和約》的制定，致力美國獨立運動，參加《獨立宣言》、《美國憲法》的制定，推行廢除黑奴的奴隸制度，或是成為美國第一位駐法大使，他都是貢獻卓著的政治家、享譽國際的外交家。

沒有不勞而獲的人生

一七九〇年四月十七日，富蘭克林與世長辭，為他精彩的人生畫下一個平凡的句點，他的墓誌銘上寫著「印刷工人班傑明·富蘭克林」，展現出他謙遜不忘本的態度。他謹守人生的十三條守則，確實不虛度人生的一分一秒，為後人留下可遵循的榜樣：

1 節制。食不過飽，飲酒不過量。

2 慎言。言則於人於己有益，不做無益閒聊。

3 秩序。各樣東西放在一定地方，各項日常事務應有一定的處理時間。

4 果斷。事情當做必做，持之以恆。

5 儉樸。花錢須於人於己有益，絕不浪費。

6 勤勉。珍惜光陰，每時每刻做有用之事。

7 誠懇。以誠待人，言必有中。

8 正直。不惡意中傷他人，不謀私利。

9 中庸。寬大為懷，避免極端。

10 整潔。穿著整潔，生活衛生。

11 冷靜。處變不驚，臨危不亂。

12 貞潔。珍重名譽，潔身自愛。

13 謙虛。以耶穌和蘇格拉底為榜樣，勿恃才而驕，要謙遜待人。

聽富蘭克林說窮理查

當我還是一個小孩子的時候，就很喜歡閱讀了，
所以老是把零用錢花在買書和蒐集書籍上……

因為對書籍感興趣，
所以後來父親決定將我培養成一個印刷工人，
當時我哥哥詹姆士已經在從事印刷工作了。
一七一七那一年，詹姆士從英國回來，
並帶回一臺印刷機和一副鉛字模，準備在波士頓開辦一間小印刷廠。
對我來說，這當然遠勝過父親的職業，
不過我內心依舊嚮往著航海生活，
而父親為了防止我將夢想變成現實，
立刻叫我去跟著兄長當學徒。

雖然也曾抗拒了一小段時間，

最後我還是被他說服去跟詹姆士簽師徒契約。

當時我只有十二歲，

按照我們簽的契約，我的學徒生涯得持續到二十一歲，

而且只有在最後一年才能領到一個專業從業人員應有的薪水。

但我只用了很短的時間就熟練所有的技術，

成為兄長的得力幫手。

一七三二年，我以理查・三德氏為名第一次出版了自己編寫的年曆，

後來我又連續編了二十五年，

現在人們大都管它叫做《窮理查年鑑》。

我努力將每一年的年曆編得實用而且充滿趣味，

所以風行一時，每年的銷售量都超過一萬本，我也從中獲得了豐厚的利潤。

《窮理查年鑑》在一般百姓之間擁有很多讀者，

整個殖民地境內幾乎都可以看得到它的身影。

當時人們除了曆書其實就很少再買其他的書籍了，

所以我認為這是一個很適合教育百姓們的重要工具。

我把格言印在年曆每頁之間的空白處，

這些格言的內容主要在指引人們勤奮、節儉，累積財富，並進一步培養一些美德。

因為，對一個窮困的人來說，要求他堅持不變地保持誠實廉潔是很困難的，

正如一句諺語所說：「空布袋很難站得直。」

這些格言包含著來自不同時代和許多民族的智慧，

後來我還把它們全都搜集在一塊兒，

以一位智慧老者在商品拍賣會上向人們發表演說的形式，

編寫成一篇前後連貫的演講詞，

以這樣的方式將所有的建議集中起來，在人們心中留下了更深刻的印象。

我把這篇文章放在一七五八年年曆的卷首，受到相當多人的讚賞，

而且歐洲大陸幾乎所有的報紙都轉載了它。

在法國，它還出了兩種譯本；

在英國，這些格言更是被印在大幅的紙張上，張貼在家中；

傳教士和地主們大量訂購，免費贈送給貧苦的教友和佃農。

我的格言勸導人們不要無謂地砸大錢去購買進口奢侈品，

至此之後的數年，當人們看到在賓夕法尼亞累積愈來愈多財富的時候，

有不少人認為是《窮理查年鑑》產生的影響力。

——摘自《從卑微到偉大的富蘭克林》

B. Franklin

Contents

Part2 窮理查教你比別人更成功 085

誰是**窮埋查**？

窮理查是誰？人們常問起，他住在哪裡？做什麼生意？卻從未能知悉。為了解答各位的好奇，且讓我簡略介紹我的夫人和我自己。感謝仁慈的讀者，和我無微不至的髮妻，讓我幸福無比，生活如意。我靠寫作維生；她則忙草地排水的生意，或是為貧瘠的小丘蓋上陰影遮蔽（譯註：指妻子常發脾氣）。用犁深耕肥沃土，好讓穀倉裝穀物。從我豐收果樹釀玉液，釀我甜奶油，造我乾起司。

我們都讀過一些書，但只有少數才讓智慧和機智匯集在一處；讓好品德有目共睹，教導我們什麼是真理，什麼是正途。真誠的朋友，正直的友人，讓我們的人生經常充滿歡樂氣氛。我們的桌椅整潔，三餐簡樸；常開門戶招待羞赧的貧戶。沒有宴會狂熱的激情，我們喜愛關心社會福祉的來賓。我們也不聽從迷信與傳說，那只會欺騙人們一錯再錯。我們不會墨守成規，偽善的教條只會讓良知無從跟隨。當愚昧無知掩住了可疑界線，在那善惡交錯的灰色邊界；我們不辨是非衝動冒險，一頭栽進未知的黑暗深淵。如果做對，也要當心；如果做錯，要下決心不讓這條毒蛇繼續盤據在心。細察手段動機和目的；改正我們自己，至少也要有改善的努力。

我們的靈魂坦蕩蕩，我們的目標公平而正當，不是為虛榮，也不是偽善；成功時，滿懷感激；失敗時，受懲罰也甘之如飴；懷抱希望，相信上帝。

——《窮理查年鑑》一七四六年

part 1

窮理查教你變
有錢人

可敬的讀者：

　　我聽說，對於一名作家來說，沒有什麼樂趣能比發現自己的作品受到其他飽學之士所引用來得更大了。我很難得享受到這等樂趣，因為（容我大言不慚）儘管我是這四分之一世紀中最傑出的年曆作家，不知道出於什麼樣的理由，其他的同行作家卻都很吝於給我掌聲，所以幾乎沒有其他作家注意到我，使我的作品並未帶給我實質收益，而乏人讚賞則經常消磨我的志氣。

　　所以我歸納出，人們才是我能力的最佳裁判，因為他們會買我的著作；而且，在我徬徨無依、還未廣為人知的時候，就經常聽到有人這樣講：「就像窮理查說的一樣⋯⋯」這給我極大的安慰，因為這不只證明我的說法被重視，還證明了對我身為作者的看重。為了激勵我自己記得重複那些睿智的話語，我偶爾也非常慎重地引用我自己的語句。

　　所以您應該可以看出，對於接下來要向您說的這件事，我內心有多麼感激！我最近去了聚集著一大群人的貨物拍賣場。拍賣的時刻還沒到，人們正討論著時局有多差，其中有一個人叫住了一位乾淨體面的白髮老頭，「唉呦，亞伯拉罕老爹，您覺得眼下這時局怎麼樣？抽這麼高的稅，是不是要把整個國家都給毀了？咱們又怎麼繳得起這稅金呢？您說說咱們該怎麼辦吧？」

　　亞伯拉罕老爹站了起來，答道：「如果你們要聽俺的勸，俺就簡單講講，因為就像窮理查說的一樣，對聰明的人只要講半句話就夠了，話再多也裝不滿籮筐。」其他人圍了過來，拱著他，要他暢所欲言，他接著說道：「各位親朋好友，這稅的確抽得很重，要是政府公佈的那些是我們唯一要付的錢，咱們還有許多東西得清，而且對咱們之中有些人來說還更重得多。咱們可以很容易就付清了；但咱們之中有些人來說還更重得多。咱們要為自己的驕傲付出三倍，為自己的愚蠢付出四倍，而這些稅並不是牧師說赦免咱們就能輕易解除的。不過，咱們可以聽聽可能對咱們有好處的好建議；就像窮理查在他一七三三年的年曆裡頭說的，**天助自助者**。

政府要是強徵人民花十分之一的時間為他們做事，咱們都會覺得太苛刻，但懶散卻占了咱們更多的時間，如果算算花在徹底怠惰、啥都不做的時間，還有花在無謂的事情或消遣上頭的時間，東扣西減，咱們就沒剩多少了。怠惰會使人生病，所以絕對會讓人短命。就像窮理查說的，**懶惰就像鐵鏽，比勞動耗損得更多；鑰匙若常用，光亮不生鏽。**

但是窮理查也說，**你若愛惜性命，不要浪費光陰；點滴的光陰，累積成生命。**咱們花在睡覺的時間比咱們需要的還多太多啦！都忘了窮理查說過，**睡著的狐狸抓不著雞，又說，墳裡頭有得你睡。**要是光陰是最寶貴的東西，那麼浪費光陰，就像窮理查說的一樣，**是最奢侈的揮霍**，因為他在別的地方說過，**時光一去不復回；還說，我們總是認為時間充足，但事實證明總是不夠。**

咱們該起而行，有目的而行——勤奮才能減少問題產生。就像窮理查說的，**怠惰讓事**

情困難，勤奮使事情簡單；人若起得晚，整天都匆忙，盡量別把工作留到晚上。懶散走得有夠慢，貧困隨即就追上。就像俺在窮理查年曆中讀到的一樣，他還說，管好你的生意，別讓生意駕馭你；早睡又早起，讓你聰明健康又富裕。

所以何必期盼時局變好？如果咱們努力些，就能讓時局變好了。就像窮理查說的，勤奮不必靠希望，靠希望過活，餓死在街頭。不勞無獲！雙手啊，爭個氣，因為俺還沒土地，不過要是俺有土地，就得被課重稅了。

還有啊，窮理查也同樣說了：有一技在身，就有地位身分；有一份事業，就有收入和尊嚴。但是這一技之長，一定得要發揮；這份事業，一定要發展，不然既沒有地位，也沒有收入讓咱們繳得起稅。如果我們夠勤奮，就絕不會捱餓，因為就像窮理查說的，勤奮人家的廳堂，飢餓只能偷觀望，不敢進門來閒晃。收稅員和警察也不會進門來，因為窮理查說，勤奮能償債，絕望只會債滾債。

儘管你沒有發現寶藏，也沒有親戚留給你龐大遺產，但就像窮理查說的，勤勉是幸運之母。努力勤勉，上帝就賜你一切恩典。窮理查也說，趁著懶人還夢酣，下田努力忙深耕，就有豐富的收成，夠你銷售與貯存。把握今天好好做，因為不知道明天又有什麼礙著你的事頭，這也就是為什麼窮理查說，一個今天值得兩個明天；又說，什麼事情明天該做，今日就先做。你要是個僕人，被主人發現你在偷懶，難道不會感到丟臉嗎？所以你就該是你自己的主人，因為窮理查說，發現自己在偷懶，你得自慚。既然為自己、為家人、為國家、為國王有那麼多事情得做，最好天才剛亮就開始動手，別讓太陽低頭說，這裡躺個懶惰蟲。親手拿起工具做事，別忘了窮理查說過，**貓兒穿襪套，老鼠捉不到**。

要做的事可能真的太多，你也可能手無縛雞之力，但是持續努力，終究能有好成績，因為滴水能穿石，勤勉有耐心，老鼠咬斷粗鋼筋；就像窮理查在俺忘了是哪一年的年曆裡頭說的，**只要工夫深，小刀鏟斷老樹根**。

俺好像聽到你們有人說，人難道就不能享受享受？俺告訴你，老弟，窮理查說了，**想要有閒暇享受，時間就得好好利用**；他還說，**連一分鐘都沒把握，千萬別放過一個鐘頭**。

休閒時間，就是利用時間做點有用的事；這是勤快人物的享受，懶漢還沒這福分呢！所以窮理查說了，**閒暇生活和懶散生活是兩回事**。難道你能想像懶惰居然能比勤勞給你帶來更多舒服的享受？不會的，因為就像窮理查說的，**勞累來自安逸，麻煩源於懶散**。四體若不勤，人們只能靠靠小聰明，但是他們可沒真材實料來經營。不過勤奮倒是能帶來享受、財富和尊敬；遠離享樂，它們就會追著你。**好的紡紗工，輪班時間長；我今有牛又有羊，大伙兒都說我此後運道旺**──窮理查說的這些真是對極了。

但是講勤奮以外，同樣還得堅持、努力、細心，好好用咱的眼睛看管咱家自己的事情，別太相信其他人；因為窮理查說過，**從來不曾親眼目睹，經常移植的樹木，或是經常搬遷的家族，能繁衍得像定居者一樣富庶**。

同樣，搬家三次，糟得像是失火一次。還有，管好你生意，你的生意就能養活你。還有，想把事情完成就動手，不想完成就送走。再來，莊稼人想豐收，自己就得拉犁走。

還有，大師的眼睛，比他雙手更辛勤；以及欠缺關懷，會比欠缺知識帶來更多傷害。

此外，不去監督手下勞工，就是拿你的錢包給他們打秋風。太信賴他人的細心，反害了許多人，因為就像年曆裡說的，人在世間要能免除事情，不是靠信心，而是靠著沒信心。但對自己的細心倒有利可圖，因為窮迪克說，勤學的人有學問，仔細的人有財富，英勇的人有力量，有德的人上天堂。又說，你要想有像你一樣的好奴僕，那就為自己服務。

此外，他也建議，即使是對再小的事情，也得謹慎小心，因為有時候一失足成千古恨。再加上：少了釘子，馬蹄鐵就掉了；少了馬蹄鐵，馬兒就輸了；少了馬兒，騎士就迷路了！要是被敵人打倒，給敵人殺了，都得算在沒注意到馬蹄鐵上那根釘子頭上。

老弟們哪，對於勤勉和注意自己的事的建議就有這麼多；但還要再加上節儉這條，才能讓勤勉更保證成功。要是一個人不知怎麼保存他的所得，就是拉著自己的人生去推石磨，最後還是死得連頭羊都不值。就像窮理查說的，廚房太大間，意志最不堅。而且——入不敷出好常見，因為女人寧可泡茶閒聊天，不願動動針黹好賺錢，男人為了酒中仙，不願披荊斬棘去墾田。

你要想有錢，他在另一本年曆裡頭說啦，多想著省錢，別顧著賺錢：印度也沒讓西班牙致富，因為她的收入還不夠她的支出。所以趕緊遠離你那些花大錢的蠢事，就不會有這麼多閒工夫抱怨時局不好啦、稅賦重啦、一家老小嗷嗷待哺了。因為就像窮迪克說的，美色與美酒，賭博與詐欺，會讓財富貶低，慾望無底。

而且啊，一個惡習不除掉，馬上兩個來報到。你也許會想，偶爾來點茶、喝杯酒、吃點昂貴的、穿點漂亮的、三不五時找點樂子，這不是什麼大不了的事；但是記著窮理查說的話，積少成多啊！還有留心小筆開銷，小裂縫也能讓大船沉掉。又說，挑剔的人愛什麼，問問乞丐最知道。另外還有，傻子做菜忙，卻讓智者吃得香。

你們大伙兒都到這服裝飾品拍賣場。你說那些是好東西，但要是不小心，可能對你來說都是壞東西。你們想要這東西賣得便宜，甚至比成本還低，但你若沒機會穿上這些東西，它們就都賣得太貴。記得窮理查的話，買了不需要的，到頭來就得賣你的必需品了；還有，要撿便宜，得先暫停。他意思是，這椿便宜可能只是表面上的，實際上並非如此；否則成交後就只能讓你勒緊褲帶，無益有害。就像他說，很多人因撿了便宜而受害。

窮理查又說，花錢買了令人後悔的東西，真是傻兮兮；但這種蠢事在拍賣場裡天天上演，因為人們都沒注意到年曆裡的提醒。就像窮理查說的，智者從別人受到的傷害裡學習，傻瓜卻很少從他們自己受的傷裡得到教訓；但是呢，能從別人的傷害學到教訓的人，才叫有福氣。很多人哪，為了想要打扮得漂漂亮亮，只能活活餓死，還讓一家大小吃不飽；就像窮理查說的，絲織品和麻布、棉布和天絲絨，都會撲滅房的爐火。這些不是生活必需品，也很少能叫它們便利品，但是光只是因為它們看起來漂亮，就不知道讓多少人想要擁有這些東西。

人工造成的需求，比天生的還要更多；就像窮理查說的，**一個窮人百樣缺**。為了這些，以及其他的奢侈品，上流名門也會變得窮困，被迫要向他們從前瞧不起，但卻勤奮節儉，努力掙錢的人來借錢——這種情況根本就像窮理查說的一樣，**農夫站得直挺挺，高過貴族屈膝伏地**。或許他們有著祖傳的一塊小土地，或者根本不知道來自哪裡，但他們想著太陽永遠不下山，白日不會變黑暗，所以那麼一點小小花費，根本不值得在意（就像窮理查說的，**小孩子和傻子會以為二十先令和二十年，沒有花完的一天**），但是一直從餐盤裡頭拿取，又不放進去，很快就見底；所以就像窮迪克說的，**直到水井乾涸，才知道水的價值幾何**。可是他們要是接受他的建議，老早就曉得這件事了。

想要知道錢的價值，去借點錢試試，因為去借錢就是去傷心；而確實要是有人借錢給這種人，當他去找他們的時候就是去收錢。窮迪克老爹建議說，**愛慕虛榮的確是種空虛的詛咒；你要是迷戀任何風潮，最好先看看你的荷包。**

而且，驕傲和欠缺同樣是乞丐，但是要錢要得更厲害。你要是買了一件好東西，就得再多買十件，才能讓你有整套的外貌；然而窮迪克說了，**克制第一個慾望，比滿足隨之而來的慾望容易。**所以窮人想要學有錢人，真是蠢事一樁，好比是青蛙吸口氣，就以為自己跟牛一樣肥了。

蝴蝶是什麼？頂多是隻毛蟲打扮過。裝扮俗麗的公子哥兒，與他的畫像正符合。

真的是瘋了才會為了這些奢侈品躲債！

我們在這個拍賣場裡，有六個月的時間可以延後付款，這可能吸引了我們之中某些人的注意，因為我們沒法兒拽著錢不用，想要馬上就花光。但是啊，想想看當你躲債的時候你做了什麼——你是讓其他人的權力壓過了你的自由。如果你不按時付錢，就會愧對於你的債主；你對他講話的時候就會感到害怕；你會編一些可憐兮兮的爛理由，最後丟掉你的誠信，沉淪到無恥謊話說不停。因為就像窮理查說的，**第一等惡事是躲債，第二就是說謊**。

還有，**謊言騎在債務背上走**。可是生而自由的英國人不應該在見到人或是和人說話的時候感到害羞或害怕。

窮困往往會剝奪人的精神和美德——窮理查說得好，**空布袋很難站起來。**

你對下令禁止你打扮得像個紳士或淑女，不然就囚禁起來或是做奴隸的國王或政府會有什麼感想？你難道不會說你生而自由，有權照你高興打扮，這道法令侵害了你的權利，這樣的政府是個暴虐的政體？然而，你如果為了這些衣服躲債，你就是讓自己陷入那樣的暴政！

要是你還不起錢，你的債主可以隨他高興，剝奪你的自由，使你終生受限，不然就是把你賣了當奴隸！要是標到了商品，你或許對這筆錢沒有多想，然而窮理查告訴我們，**債主的記憶力比債務人高明**；在別的地方又說，**債主都屬於某個迷信教派，恪守還債期限的到來**。還債的日子在你注意之前就已經逼近了，在你能夠還債之前，債主就來提醒了。

你要是記著你的債務，那期限雖然乍看起來很長，但一開始減少，卻短得不得了。到時看來，時間不只在肩膀上有翅膀，腳跟也加了一雙。窮理查說過，**想要短期借貸，借他時別忘了復活節時催還債**。而既然向人借錢是當出借人的奴隸，債務人是債權人的奴隸，就得跟窮理查說的一樣，**快避開枷鎖，維護你的自由，才能維持你的獨立——勤奮、節儉、有自由**。

你們現在也許會覺得自己處在富裕的環境，所以可以稍微浪費一點沒關係，但就像窮理查說的，**為了年歲和必需品，盡量儲蓄沒關係；朝陽再亮遲早也落西**。

收入可能短暫又不穩定，但是只要你還活著，支出就很固定了；就像窮理查說的，**比起不讓一支煙囪熄火，蓋兩支煙囪要容易得多**。所以寧可沒吃晚飯就上床，也不要為了躲債滾下床。就像窮理查說的，**盡量拿，拿了就緊握；這可是將鉛變黃金的那種石頭**。

你有了賢者之石，就不要再抱怨時局不好，還是什麼稅賦太高。

老弟們啊，這就是理性與智慧的教訓哪，但是你也不要太依賴自己的努力、節儉跟明智，因為儘管這些是好東西，若沒有上天的保佑，這些都會枯萎；所以要謙卑地祈求老天保佑，不要刻薄地對待沒有這福氣的人，反而要安慰、幫助他們。要記得約伯也曾經受苦，之後才又興旺富足。

現在來做個總結，經驗是間好學校，但是傻瓜不會再上其他的學校，而且很少在學校；因為我們真的就像窮理查說的，只能夠提供建議，卻不能幫人處理。不過呢，記住一點，窮理查說過：**聽不進建議，就沒有人幫你。況且，如果你不聽理性的忠告，她就踹你膝蓋骨。**」

那位老紳士就這樣結束他的精彩演說。在場的人聽了，也都贊同這番道理，可是馬上就做出相反的事情，就像這只是場一般的講道而已──因為拍賣一開始，他們就又開始大買特買，不管那老人的告誡，還有他們自己對稅賦的恐懼。

我想那位老人一定徹底研究過我的年曆，消化了我散佈在這二十五年裡的各項主題。他對我的頻頻指名一定刺激到其他人，但我的虛榮卻對此感到極度高興，雖然我自覺到我的智慧並不到他對我誇讚的十分之一，只是從各朝各代、各國各地中，拾人牙慧而已。不過，我決定要變得更好，才能對這份誇讚有所回報；儘管我原本打算買件新外套，我決定馬上回頭，再多穿穿我的舊外套。讀者們，如果您也這麼做，收穫就會同我一樣多。

——《窮理查年鑑》一七五八年．〈財富之路〉

李嘉誠（香港知名企業家）

富蘭克林這本著作一紙風行，成為除《聖經》外最暢銷的書……在〈財富之路〉一文內，富蘭克林清楚簡單地說明，勤奮、小心、儉樸、穩健是致富之核心態度。

The WAY to Wealth,

AND

A PLAN by which every MAN MAY PAY HIS TAXES.

Courteous Reader,

I HAVE heard that nothing gives an author ſo great pleaſure as to find his works reſpectfully quoted by others. Judge, then, how much I muſt have been gratified by an incident I am going to relate to you. I ſtopped my horſe lately, where a great number of people were collected at an auction of merchants goods. The hour of ſale not being come, they were converſing on the badneſs of the times, and one of the company called to a plain clean Old Man, with white locks,——'Pray, *Father Abraham*, what think you of the times? Will not theſe heavy taxes quite ruin the country? How ſhall we be ever able to pay them? What would you adviſe us to?' Father Abraham ſtood up, and replied, 'If you would have my advice, I will give it you in ſhort, "for a word to the wiſe is enough," as *Poor Richard* ſays.' They joined in deſiring him to ſpeak his mind, and gathering round him, he proceeded as follows:

'Friend, ſays he, the taxes are indeed very heavy; and if thoſe laid on by the government were the only ones we had to pay, we might more eaſily diſcharge them; but we have many others, and much more grievous to ſome of us. We are taxed twice as much by our idleneſs, three times as much by our pride, and four times as much by our folly; and from theſe taxes the commiſſioners cannot eaſe or deliver us, by allowing an abatement. However, let us hearken to good advice, and ſomething may be done for us; "God helps them that help themſelves," as Poor Richard ſays.'

I. 'It would be thought a hard government that ſhould tax its people one tenth part of their time, to be employed in its ſervice: but idleneſs taxes many of us much more; ſloth, by bringing on diſeaſes, abſolutely ſhortens life. "Sloth, like ruſt, conſumes faſter than labour wears; while the uſed key is always bright," as Poor Richard ſays.—"But doſt thou love life, then do not ſquander time, for that is the ſtuff life is made of," as Poor Richard ſays. 'How much more than is neceſſary do we ſpend in ſleep; forgetting that "The ſleeping fox catches no poultry, and that there will be ſleeping enough in the grave," as Poor Richard ſays.

"If time be of all things the moſt precious, waſting time muſt be," as Poor Richard ſays, "the greateſt prodigality;" ſince, as he elſewhere tells us, "Loſt time is never found again; and what we call time enough, always proves little enough:" Let us then up and be doing, and doing to the purpoſe; for by diligence we ſhall do more with leſs perplexity. "Sloth makes all things difficult, but induſtry all eaſy; and, he that riſeth late, muſt trot all day, and ſhall ſcarce overtake his buſineſs at night; while lazineſs travels ſo ſlowly, that poverty ſoon overtakes him. Drive thy buſineſs, let not that drive thee; and early to bed, and early to riſe, makes a man healthy, wealthy, and wiſe," as Poor Richard ſays.

'So what ſignifies wiſhing and hoping for better times? We may make theſe times better, if we beſtir ourſelves. "Induſtry need not wiſh, and he that lives upon hope will die faſting. There are no gains without pains; then help hands, for I have no lands," or, if I have, they are ſmartly taxed. He that hath a trade, hath an eſtate; and he that hath a calling, hath an office of profit and honour," as Poor Richard ſays; but then the trade muſt be worked at, and the calling well followed, or neither the eſtate nor the office will enable us to pay our taxes. If we are induſtrious we ſhall never ſtarve; for, "at the working man's houſe hunger looks in, but dares not enter." Nor will the bailiff or the conſtable enter, for, "Induſtry pays debts, while deſpair encreaſeth them." What though you have found no treaſure, nor has any rich relation left you a legacy, "Diligence is the mother of good luck, and God gives all things to induſtry. Then plow deep, while ſluggards ſleep, and you ſhall have corn to ſell and to keep." Work while it is called to-day, for you know not how much you may be hindered to-morrow. "One to-day is worth two to-morrows," as Poor Richard ſays; and farther, Never leave that till to-morrow, which you can do to-day."—If you were a ſervant, would you not be aſhamed that a good maſter ſhould catch you idle? Are you then your own maſter? Be aſhamed to catch yourſelf idle, when there is ſo much to be done for yourſelf, your family, and your country.——Handle your tools without mittens; remember, that "The cat in gloves catches no mice," as Poor Richard ſays. It is true, there is much to be done, and, perhaps, you are weak handed; but ſtick to it ſteadily, and you will ſee great effects; for "Conſtant dropping wears away ſtones; and by diligence and patience the mouſe ate in two the cable; and little ſtrokes fell great oaks."

'Methinks I hear ſome of you ſay, "Muſt a man afford himſelf no leiſure?" I will tell thee, my friend, what Poor Richard ſays; "Employ thy time well, if thou meaneſt to gain leiſure, and, ſince thou art not ſure of a minute, throw not away an hour." *Leiſure* is time for doing ſomething uſeful; this leiſure the diligent man will obtain, but the lazy man never; for, "A life of leiſure, and a life of lazineſs are two things. Many, without labour, would live by their wits only, but they break for want of ſtock;" whereas induſtry gives comfort, and plenty, and reſpect. "Fly pleaſures, and they will follow you. The diligent ſpinner has a large ſhift; and now I have a ſheep and a cow, every body bids me good-morrow."

II. 'But with our induſtry we muſt likewiſe be ſteady, ſettled, and careful, and overſee our own affairs with our own eyes, and not truſt too much to others; for as Poor Richard ſays,

"I never ſaw an oft removed tree,
Nor yet an oft removed family,
That throve ſo well as thoſe that ſettled be."

'And again, "Three removes is as bad as a fire;" and again, "Keep thy ſhop, and thy ſhop will keep thee;" and again, "If you would have your buſineſs done, go; if not, ſend." And again,

"He that by the plough would thrive,
Himſelf muſt either hold or drive."

'And again, "The eye of a maſter will do more work than both his hands;" and again, "Want of care does us more damage than want of knowledge;" and again, "Not to overſee workmen, is to leave them your purſe open; truſting too much to others care is the ruin of many;" for, "In the affairs of this world, men are ſaved, not by faith, but by the want of it:" But a man's *own* care is profitable; for, "If you would have a faithful ſervant, and one that you like, ſerve yourſelf. A little neglect may breed great miſchief; for want of a nail the ſhoe was loſt; for want of a ſhoe the horſe was loſt; and for want of a horſe the rider was loſt," being overtaken and ſlain by the enemy; all for want of a little care about a horſe-ſhoe nail."

III. 'So much for induſtry, my friends, and attention to one's own buſineſs; but to theſe we muſt add frugality, if we would make our induſtry more certainly ſucceſsful. A man may, if he knows not how to ſave as he gets, "keep his noſe all his life to the grindſtone, and die not worth a groat at laſt. A fat kitchen makes a lean will;" and

"Many eſtates are ſpent in the getting,
Since women for tea forſook ſpinning and
knitting,
And men for punch forſook hewing and
ſplitting."

"If you would be wealthy, think of ſaving, as well as of getting. The Indies have not made Spain rich, becauſe her outgoes are greater than her incomes."

'Away, then, with your expenſive follies, and you will not then have ſo much cauſe to complain of hard times, heavy taxes, and chargeable families; for

"Women and wine, game and deceit,
Make the wealth ſmall, and the want great."

'And farther, "What maintains one vice, would bring up two children." You may think, perhaps, that a little tea, or a little punch now and then, diet a little more coſtly, cloaths a little finer, and a little entertainment now and then, can be no great matter; but remember, "Many a little makes a mickle." Beware of little expences; "A ſmall leak will ſink a great ſhip," as Poor Richard ſays; and again, "Who dainties love, ſhall beggars prove;" and moreover, "Fools make feaſts, and wiſe men eat them." Here you are all got together to this ſale of fineries and nick-nacks. You call them *goods*; but, if you do not take care, they will prove *evils* to ſome of you. You expect they will be ſold cheap, and, perhaps, they may for leſs than they coſt; but, if you have no occaſion for them, they muſt be dear to you. Remember what Poor Richard ſays, "Buy what thou haſt no need of, and ere long thou ſhalt ſell thy neceſſaries." And again, "At a great pennyworth pauſe awhile." He means, that perhaps the cheapneſs is apparent only, and not real; or the bargain, by ſtraitening thee in thy buſineſs, may do thee more harm than good. For in another place he ſays, "Many have been ruined by buying good pennyworths." Again, "It is fooliſh to lay out money in a purchaſe of repentance;" and yet this folly is practiſed every day at auctions, for want of minding the Almanack. Many a one, for the ſake of finery on the back, has gone with a hungry belly, and half ſtarved their families; "Silks and ſattins, ſcarlets and velvets, put out the kitchen fire," as Poor Richard ſays. Theſe are not the neceſſaries of life; they can ſcarcely be called the conveniencies; and yet only becauſe they look pretty, how many want to have them? By theſe, and other extravagances, the genteel are reduced to poverty, and forced to borrow of thoſe whom they formerly deſpiſed, but who, through induſtry and frugality, have maintained their ſtanding; in which caſe it appears plainly that "A ploughman on his legs, is higher than a gentleman on his knees," as Poor Richard ſays.——Perhaps they have had a ſmall eſtate left them, which they knew not the getting of; they think "It is day, and will never be night;" that a little to be ſpent out of ſo much is not worth minding; but "Always taking out of the meal-tub, and never putting in, ſoon comes to the bottom," as Poor Richard ſays; and then, "When the well is dry, they know the worth of water." But this they might have known before, if they had taken his advice: If you would know the value of money, go and try to borrow ſome; for he that goes a borrowing goes a ſorrowing," as Poor Richard ſays; and, indeed, ſo does he that lends to ſuch people, when he goes to get it in again. Poor Dick farther adviſes, and ſays,

"Fond pride of dreſs is ſure a very curſe;
Ere fancy you conſult, conſult your purſe."

'And again, "Pride is as loud a beggar as Want, and a great deal more ſaucy." When you have bought one fine thing, you muſt buy ten more, that your appearance may be all of a-piece; but Poor Dick ſays, "It is eaſier to ſuppreſs the firſt deſire, than to ſatisfy all that follow it:" And it is as truly folly for the poor to ape the rich, as for the frog to ſwell, in order to equal the ox.

"Veſſels large may venture more,
But little boats ſhould keep near ſhore."

"It is, however, a folly ſoon puniſhed:" for, as Poor Richard ſays, "Pride that dines on vanity ſups on contempt: Pride breakfaſted with plenty, dined with poverty, and ſupped with infamy." And, after all, of what uſe is this pride of appearance, for which ſo much is riſked, ſo much is ſuffered? It cannot promote health, nor eaſe pain; it makes no increaſe of merit in the perſon, it creates envy, it haſtens misfortune.

'But what madneſs muſt it be to *run in debt* for theſe ſuperfluities? We are offered, by the terms of this ſale, ſix months credit; and that, perhaps, has induced ſome of us to attend it, becauſe we cannot ſpare the ready money, and hope now to be fine without it. But ah! think what you do when you run in debt; you give to another power over your liberty. If you cannot pay at the time, you will be aſhamed to ſee your creditor; you will be in fear when you ſpeak to him; you will make poor, pitiful, ſneaking excuſes, and, by degrees, come to loſe your veracity, and ſink into baſe downright lying; for "The *ſecond* vice is lying, the firſt is running in debt," as Poor Richard ſays; and again to the ſame purpoſe, "Lying rides upon Debt's back;" whereas a free born American ought not to be aſhamed nor afraid to ſee or ſpeak to any man living. But poverty often deprives a man of all ſpirit and virtue.' "It is hard for an empty bag to ſtand upright." 'What would you think of that prince, or of that government, who ſhould iſſue an edict forbidding you to dreſs like a gentleman or gentlewoman, on pain of impriſonment or ſervitude? Would you not ſay that you were free, have a right to dreſs as you pleaſe, and that ſuch an edict would be a breach of your privileges, and ſuch a government tyrannical? And yet you are about to put yourſelf under that tyranny, when you run in debt for ſuch dreſs! Your creditor has authority, at his pleaſure, to deprive you of your liberty, by confining you in gaol for life, or by ſelling you for a ſervant, if you ſhould not be able to pay him. When you have got your bargain, you may, perhaps, think little of payment; but as Poor Richard ſays, "Creditors have better memories than debtors; creditors are a ſuperſtitious ſect, great obſervers of ſet days and times." The day comes round before you are aware, and the demand is made before you are prepared to ſatisfy it; or, if you bear your debt in mind, the term which at firſt ſeemed ſo long, will, as it leſſens, appear extremely ſhort. Time will ſeem to have added wings to his heels as well as his ſhoulders. "Thoſe have a ſhort Lent who owe money to be paid at Eaſter." At preſent, perhaps, you may think yourſelves in thriving circumſtances, and that you can bear a little extravagance without injury: but

"For age and want ſave while you may,
No morning ſun laſts a whole day."

'Gain may be temporary and uncertain, but ever, while you live, expence is conſtant and certain; and, "It is eaſier to build two chimneys, than to keep one in fuel," as Poor Richard ſays: So, "Rather go to bed ſupperleſs than riſe in debt."

"Get what you can, and what you get hold,
'Tis the ſtone that will turn all your lead
into gold."

'And when you have got the philoſopher's ſtone, ſure you will no longer complain of bad times or the difficulty of paying taxes.'

IV. 'This doctrine, my friends, is reaſon and wiſdom: But, after all, do not depend too much upon your own induſtry and frugality and prudence, though excellent things; for they may all be blaſted without the bleſſing of heaven; and, therefore, aſk that bleſſing humbly, and be not uncharitable to thoſe that at preſent ſeem to want it, but comfort and help them. Remember Job ſuffered, and was afterwards proſperous.

'And now, to concukle, "Experience keeps a dear ſchool, but fools will learn in no other," as Poor Richard ſays, and ſcarce in that; for, it is true, "We may give advice, but we cannot give conduct:" However, remember this, "They that will not be counſelled, cannot be helped;" and further, that "If you will not hear Reaſon, ſhe will ſurely rap your knuckles," as Poor Richard ſays.'

Thus the old gentleman ended his harangue. The people heard it, and approved the doctrine, and immediately practiſed the contrary, juſt as if it had been a common ſermon; for the auction opened, and they began to buy extravagantly——I found the good man had thoroughly ſtudied my Almanacks, and digeſted all I had dropt on theſe topics during the courſe of twenty-five years. The frequent mention he made of me muſt have tired any one elſe; but my vanity was wonderfully delighted with it, though I was conſcious, that not a tenth part of the wiſdom was my own, which he aſcribed to me; but rather the gleanings that I had made of the ſenſe of all ages and nations. However, I reſolved to be the better for the echo of it; and, though I had at firſt determined to buy ſtuff for a new coat, I went away, reſolved to wear my old one a little longer. Reader, if thou wilt do the ſame, thy profit will be as great as mine. I am, as ever,

Thine to ſerve thee,

RICHARD SAUNDERS.

Philadelphia: Printed by DANIEL HUMPHREYS, in Spruce-ſtreet, near the Drawbridge.

輕輕的荷包，是重重的詛咒。
荷包一輕，心裡添重擔。
曾是窮人不丟臉，覺得這事兒丟
臉才丟臉。

窮理查說……

「時間就是金錢。」

1　難道你還沒有為標靶做上標記？還是像個追著烏鴉的男孩，拿著彈弓和石頭，一棵樹追過一棵樹，毫無收穫，徒讓光陰虛度？

Hast thou no mark at which to bend thy bow? Or like a boy pursu'st the carrion crow with pellets and with stones, from tree to tree. A fruitless toil, and liv'st extempore?

2　失去金錢讓人憂，被搶被騙令人怒，但失去的金錢可能找得回，被搶的東西可能會復原，而寶貴的時光一旦失去就再也追不回，但我們還是恣意揮霍，當它毫無價值、沒用處。

3 時光一逝不復回。
Lost Time is never found again.

4 一個今天，值得兩個明天。
One To-day is worth two To-morrows.

5 天天浪費賺取四便士的時間，等於日復一日浪費每天利用一百英鎊的特權。虛度賺取五先令的光陰，白白的失去五先令，更像是把錢丟到水裡一樣地「精明」。丟掉五先令，不只失去小數目，更沒了拿錢交易的好處，累積到老，可就少了一大筆錢可舒服。

He that wastes idly a Groat's worth of his Time per Day, one Day with another, wastes the Privilege of using 100 l. each Day. He that idly loses 5 s. worth of time, loses 5 s. & might as prudently throw 5 s. in the River. He that loses 5 s. not only loses that Sum, but all the Advantage that might be made by turning it in Dealing, which by the time that a young Man becomes old, amounts to a comfortable Bag of Mony. (編註：Groat為英國古四便士銀幣)

6 明日事，今日畢。（編註：如果可以，就盡早完成工作）

Have you somewhat to do to-morrow; do it to-day.

7 你若愛惜性命，不要浪費光陰；點滴的光陰，累積成生命。

Dost thou love Life? then do not squander Time; for that's the Stuff Life is made of.

8 早上睡過頭，必定整天跑著走，夜裡也很少繼續工作。

He that riseth late, must trot all day, and shall scarce overtake his business at night.

9 未經利用的空暇，不算真閒暇。
It is not Leisure that is not used.

10 想要忙裡偷閒，就要善用時間。
Employ thy time well, if thou meanest to gain leisure.

11 發現自己在發呆，要當恥辱來看待。
Be always asham'd to catch thy self idle.

12 有了時間，就別再等空閒。
If you have time dont wait for time.

13 連一分鐘都沒把握，就更別浪費整個鐘頭。
Since thou art not sure of a minute, throw not away an hour.

14 你可能會延遲，時間卻不會如此。
You may delay, but Time will not.

15 浪費光陰，不只讓外在窮困，也會使心靈貧瘠。
Prodigality of Time, produces Poverty of Mind as well as of Estate.

16 睡著的狐狸抓不著雞。快起！快快起！
The sleeping Fox catches no poultry. Up! up!

17 早睡又早起，讓你聰明、健康又富裕。
Early to bed and early to rise, makes a man healthy wealthy and wise.

18 快起來，懶惰鬼，別把生命白浪費——墳裡頭有得你睡。
Up, Sluggard, and waste not life; in the grave will be sleeping enough.

19

既然我們的時間已經有了個標準，寶貴時光已經化為鐘點計算，勤奮的人就知道應該怎麼利用每個片刻，在他們各自的專業中獲得真正的益處：虛度時光的人，事實上，就是揮霍無度的人。

Since our Time is reduced to a Standard, and the Bullion of the Day minted out into Hours, the Industrious know how to employ every Piece of Time to a real Advantage in their different Professions: And he that is prodigal of his Hours, is, in Effect, a Squanderer of Money.

祕訣 2

窮理查說：

「不勞無獲。」

1 噢，懶骨頭！你想上帝給你雙腳雙手，不是要你好好使用？

O Lazy-Bones! Dost thou think God would have given thee Arms and Legs, if he had not design'd thou should'st use them.

2 等運氣來臨的人，沒一餐有把握。

He that waits upon Fortune, is never sure of a Dinner.

3 努力勤勉，上帝賜你一切恩典。

God gives all Things to Industry.

窮理查年鑑

040

4 趁著懶人還夢酣，下田努力忙深耕，就有豐富的收成，夠你銷售與貯存。

Plough deep, while Sluggards sleep; And you shall have Corn, to sell and to keep.

5 各行翹楚，都靠著練習進步，先要有辛勤勞作，才能有將來的舒服。

In each Art Men rise but by Degrees, And Months of Labour lead to Years of Ease.

6 勤奮工作人家的廳堂，飢餓只能偷觀望，不敢進門來閒晃。

At the working man's house hunger looks in but dares not enter.

7 時光短暫，工程浩大，手下懶散，老闆催促，報酬豐厚；所以，快起身工作。

The Day is short, the Work great, the Workmen lazy, the Wages high, the Master urgeth: Up, then, and be doing

8 兢兢業業，不需許願。
Industry need not wish.

9 勤奮努力能償債，絕望只會債滾債。
Industry pays Debts, Despair encreases them.

10 勤奮、有恆又節儉，大富大貴在眼前。
Industry, Perseverance, & Frugality, make Fortune yield.

11 靠犁吃飯想興旺，不是持續做，就是拚命幹。
He that by the Plow would thrive, himself must either hold or drive.

12 期盼著收穫，就能忍苦痛。
Hope of gain Lessens pain.

13 傑克・李托播種少，收穫自然跟著少。
Jack Little sow'd little, & little he'll reap.

14 雙手啊，爭個氣！因為我還沒有土地。
Help, Hands: For I have no Lands.

窮理查說：

「懶散走得有夠慢，貧窮隨即就跟上。」

1 懶惰（就好像鐵鏽一樣）比勞動耗損更多：鑰匙若常用，光亮不生鏽。

Sloth (like Rust) consumes faster than Labour wears: the used Key is always bright.

2 悠閒生活和懶散過活，兩者不同別搞錯。

A life of leisure, and a life of laziness, are two things.

3 怠惰是最奢侈的揮霍。

4 因循怠惰是時間的小偷，年復一年，將時光都偷走，只憐憫地留下片刻，讓人去想想永生這件重大之事。

Procrastination is the Thief of Time. Year after Year it steals till all are fled, And to the Mercies of a Moment leaves The vast Concerns of an eternal Scene.

5 懶散是片死海，吞食所有美德。做事要勤奮，誘惑才沒法瞄準：呆坐不動的小鳥，是最易打中的目標。

Idleness is the Dead Sea, that swallows all Virtues: Be active in Business, that Temptation may miss her Aim: The Bird that sits, is easily shot.

6 懶惰的人是惡魔的員工；制服是破布，餐點是飢餓，酬勞是疾病。

The idle Man is the Devil's Hireling; whose Livery is Rags, whose Diet and Wages are Famine and Diseases.

7 勤能補拙，懶惰卻會讓人更笨拙。

Diligence overcomes Difficulties, Sloth makes them.

8 想領先全世界，就要從工作上做起：將上午該完成的事，延到下午才進行，不僅是糟糕的管理，還顯示出懶散的習性。

He that would be beforehand in the World, must be beforehand with his Business:

It is not only ill Management, but discovers a slothful Disposition, to do that in the

Afternoon, which should have been done in the Morning.

窮理查說：

「有一技在身，就有房子能棲身。」

1 我今有牛又有羊，大伙兒都說我此後運道旺。

Now I've a sheep and a cow, every body bids me good morrow.

2 在為了生計而學習法律、物理，或是其他學科時，儘管一開始會覺得困苦、艱難、無趣，但你要勤奮、有恆、有耐心；你學業的煩悶就會日漸散去，你的努力終究能夠成功豐收。你要贏過其他在職務上不認真、懶惰、散漫的人，成為你專業裡的翹楚。實力能帶來事業，事業能帶來財富，財富在你年事高時可以帶來光榮的退休。

In studying Law or Physick, or any other Art or Science, by which you propose

3 少年時的一技之長，會為成年帶來萬貫家財。

Useful Attainments in your Minority will procure Riches in Maturity,

4 有一技在身，就有了收益與自尊。

He that has a Trade, has an Office of Profit and Honour.

5 關於思辨或實踐的學習，在民主政體或貴族政體裡，都是財富與榮耀的天生來源。

to get your Livelihood, though you find it at first hard, difficult and unpleasing, use Diligence, Patience and Perseverance; the Irksomness of your Task will thus diminish daily, and your Labour shall finally be crowned with Success. You shall go beyond all your Competitors who are careless, idle or superficial in their Acquisitions, and be at the Head of your Profession.—Ability will command Business, Business Wealth; and Wealth an easy and honourable Retirement when Age shall require it.

Learning, whether Speculative or Practical, is, in Popular or Mixt Governments, the Natural Source of Wealth and Honour.

6 你要是鐵砧，站穩你腳跟；你要是鐵鎚，盡量用力捶。

When you're an Anvil, hold you still; When you're a Hammer, strike your Fill.

7 好的紡紗工，輪班時間長。

The good Spinner hath a large Shift.

8 管好你的店，你的店就會保住你。

Keep thy shop, & thy shop will keep thee.

9 大師的眼睛，比他雙手更辛勤。

The Master's Eye will do more Work than both his Hands.

窮理查說：

「管好你的生意，別讓生意駕馭你。」

1 東西便宜賣，就好像把店蓋在古德溫沙灘上，但是不愁沒客人。（編註：古德溫沙灘地勢險惡，傳說有逾二百艘商船沉沒於此）

Sell-cheap kept Shop on Goodwin Sands, and yet had Store of Custom.

2 事情辦得好，一回可當兩回好。

Well done, is twice done.

3 在市場中有耐心，價值一年一磅金。

Patience in Market, is worth Pounds in a Year.

4 勤學的人有學問；仔細的人有財富；英勇的人有力量；有德的人上天堂。

Learning to the Studious; Riches to the Careful; Power to the Bold; Heaven to the Virtuous.

5 朋友之間談生意，帳能算得清，契約有載明，就能維持這段友誼。

When a Friend deals with a Friend Let the Bargain be clear and well penn'd. That they may continue Friends to the End.

6 若在完工前就先付錢，花兩分錢只值一分錢。

He that pays for Work before it's done, has but a pennyworth for twopence.

7 重要的事情，要靠你自己，不要太過相信你的朋友或僕役；個人看來，朋友的保證可能太過動聽，僕人的擔保又很少會是真心。

In Things of moment, on thy self depend. Nor trust too far thy Servant or thy Friend: With private Views, thy Friend may promise fair, And Servants very seldom prove sincere.

8 不去監督手下勞工，就是拿你的錢包給他們打秋風。

Not to oversee Workmen, is to leave them your Purse open.

9 想把事情完成就動手，不想完成就送走。

If you would have your Business done, go; If not, send.

10 從來不曾親眼目睹，經常移植的樹木或經常搬遷的家族，能繁衍得像定居者一樣富庶。

I never saw an oft-transplanted tree, Nor yet an oft-removed family, That throve so well as those that settled be.

查理・蒙格（全球首富巴菲特五十年的智慧盟友）

用班傑明・富蘭克林的話來說，就是：「想把事情完成就動手，不想完成就送走。」如果你在思考問題的時候完全依賴別人，時常花錢請一些專家顧問，那麼當問題超出你那狹隘的知識領域時，你就大禍臨頭了。

窮理查年鑑

052

窮理查說：

「避免不義之財：沒有錢財，能夠彌補惡行的災害。」

1 別拿美德換富裕，別拿自由換權力。

Sell not virtue to purchase wealth, nor Liberty to purchase power.

2 不義之財，是真正的損害。

Bad Gains are truly Losses.

3 如果你明明知道是壞事，就別受愉悅所誘使，別受利益所指使，別受野心所腐蝕，別為先例而動搖意志，別受教唆而從事；你才能永遠快活度日──因為只要有良心，天天都是聖誕日。

Let no Pleasure tempt thee, no Profit allure thee, no Ambition corrupt thee, no Example sway thee, no Persuasion move thee, to do any thing which thou knowest to be Evil: So shalt thou always live jollily; for a good Conscience is a continual Christmass.

4 誠實的人不受不該他得的金錢與褒揚。

An honest Man will receive neither Money nor Praise, that is not his Due.

5 他人妻，不可戲，他人錢財不可欺。

Dally not with other Folks Women or Money.

6 人如果出賣信任，就會失去一大堆友人，而且貪錢永遠不會嫌過分。

He that sells upon trust, loses many friends, and always wants money.

7

窮困同時又誠實，（雖然很光榮）實在不是件易事⋯空布袋很難站得直，要是站得起來，一定很堅實！

Tis hard (but glorious) to be poor and honest: An empty Sack can hardly stand upright; but if it does, 'tis a stout one!

8

付利息是違背了某些人的原則，買通官員看起來也像是違反其他人的利益。

Tis against some Mens Principle to pay Interest, and seems against others Interest to pay the Principal.

9

智者索求不多，不過拿得正當，用得嚴謹，還能開心分享，心滿意足地放下。

A wise Man will desire no more, than what he may get justly, use soberly, distribute chearfully, and leave contentedly.

查理・蒙格

你不得不經常跟一些非常差勁的人打交道。但當律師能夠賺很多錢，大部分要歸功於他們。

就算你的客戶是個品德高尚的人，你要幫他應付的對手也往往是非常低劣的傢伙。這是我不再當律師的原因之一。

另一個原因是我的私慾，也是因為我的慾望才能帶來成功，讓我能去做個值得尊敬和理性的人。就像班傑明・富蘭克林說的：「空布袋很難站得直。」

10 別掠奪上帝，也別搶貧民，除非你想毀了你自己——老鷹雖然能夠從祭壇上面抓走火炭，但是那樣也會將牠的老巢全部燒乾。

Rob not God, nor the Poor, lest thou ruin thyself; the Eagle snatcht a Coal from the Altar, but it fired her Nest.

11 金錢和人類，交情屬於這一類：人類會偽造假錢幣，金錢也會讓人沒信義。

Money & Man a mutual Friendship show: Man makes false Money, Money makes Man so.

12 就算賺到全世界，失去了自己的靈魂，對人又有什麼好處？

What shall it profit a Man, if he gain the whole World, and lose his own Soul?

13 賣貨講信用，不會亂抬價，等於賺到他好像損失的本金與盈利⋯⋯也就是——買家挑信用，為貨付盈利。

He that sells upon Credit, asks a Price for what he sells, equivalent to the Principal and Interest of his Money for the Time he is like to be kept out of it: therefore he that buys upon Credit, pays Interest for what he buys.

14 災厄與興旺，是正直的試金石。

Calamity and Prosperity are the Touchstones of Integrity.

窮理查說：

「省一分錢就是賺兩分錢。」

1 懂得量入為出，就是懂得煉金術。

If you know how to spend less than you get, you have the Philosophers-Stone.

2 人若儉約，樣樣都便宜；人要奢侈，樣樣買不起。

All things are cheap to the saving, dear to the wasteful.

3 寧可沒吃晚餐就睡覺，好過沒吃早餐還得跑跑跳跳。（編註：此處的 run 喻因負債而跑路）

Rather go to bed supperless, than run in debt for a Breakfast.

4 聚少能成多。

Light Gains heavy Purses.

5 如果想要變有錢，多想著省錢，別顧著賺錢：印度也沒讓西班牙致富，因為她的收入相當於支出。

If you'd be wealthy, think of saving, more than of getting: The Indies have not made Spain rich, because her Outgoes equal her Incomes.

6 致富的訣竅，主要是在於節儉。人不可能得到同樣多的錢，但每個人都有實踐這項美德的能力。

The Art of getting Riches consists very much in THRIFT. All Men are not equally qualified for getting Money, but it is in the Power of every one alike to practise this Virtue.

7 留意小開銷，再大的船也可能因為小小的裂縫就沉掉。

Beware of little Expences, a small Leak will sink a great Ship.

查理‧蒙格

我們最好記住富蘭克林那句最有用的格言：

「再大的船也可能因為小小的裂縫就沉掉。」

這句格言的功效是很大的，因為大腦經常會錯失能沉大船的小紕漏。

8 省吃儉用累積所有，勝過花錢之後苦苦哀求。

Spare and have is better than spend and crave.

9 勿輕忽些微的損失或收穫：小土堆也能堆成山，看重每一筆小支出，別浪費事物，省下的每一錙銖，都能積累致富。

Nor trivial Loss, nor trivial Gain despise: Molehills, if often heap'd, to Mountains rise: Weigh every small Expence, and nothing waste, Farthings long sav'd, amount to Pounds at last.

10 為年歲和必需品，盡量儲蓄沒關係；朝陽再亮遲早會落西。

For Age and Want save while you may; No Morning Sun lasts a whole Day.

11 省一分錢就是賺兩分錢，每天省個一丁點兒，一年就是一大筆錢。有省就有得。積少能成多。

A Penny sav'd is Twopence clear, A Pin a day is a Groat a Year. Save & have.

Every little makes a mickle.

馬克・司古森（葛蘭德大學商學院主席）

「節儉是重要的收入來源」，他在《窮理查年鑑》裡這麼寫道。關於提倡節儉，他最有名的一句話是：「省一分錢就是賺兩分錢。」「省一分錢就是賺兩分錢」意義非常深刻的一句話。

12

如果您目前一天喝兩杯潘趣酒、葡萄酒或茶；今年接下來每天只能喝一杯。假使您現在每天只喝一杯，那就改成每隔一天喝一杯。要是您一週喝一杯，縮減到兩週喝一杯。若您的飲用量沒有隨著減少次數而增加，您在這些項目上的花費就能省下一半。

If you are now a Drinker of Punch, Wine or Tea, twice a Day; for the ensuing Year drink them but once a Day. If you now drink them but once a Day, do it but every other Day. If you do it now but once a Week, reduce the Practice to once a Fortnight. And if you do not exceed in Quantity as you lessen the Times, half your Expence in these Articles will be saved.

13

殺價還不算太丟臉，勝過鞠躬哈腰去討恩典。

'Tis less discredit to abridge petty charges, than to stoop to petty Gettings.

窮理查說：

「用錢有術才是有錢的最大好處。」

Some are justly laught at for keeping their Money foolishly, others for spending it idly; He is the greatest fool that lays it out in a purchase of repentance.

1 死抱金錢，活該被人笑；傻傻花錢，也沒比較好…天下傻瓜第一號，才會花錢買懊惱。

Tis a well spent penny that saves a groat.

2 花一毛，省四毛，這筆交易夠划算。

3 當您想買瓷器、陶器、印度絲織品，或是其他脆弱的手工藝

品，我不會對您太苛刻，要您絕對不能買。我的建議只是要
您先放下它（就像放下您的後悔一樣），來年再說──就某
些方面來說，這可以避免後悔。

When you incline to buy China Ware, Chinces, India Silks, or any other of their flimsey slight Manufactures; I would not be so hard with you, as to insist on your absolutely resolving against it all I advise, is, to put it off (as you do your Repentance) till another Year; and this, in some Respects, may prevent an Occasion of Repentance.

4 好多交易實在太可笑，雖然買家自己不知道；看看那某甲的
馬兒，還有某乙的房子，到底有多好。

There is much money given to be laught at, though the purchasers don't know it; witness A's fine horse, & B's fine house.

5 當你想買非必需的家用品，或者任何不實用的物品時，要考
慮你在世時是否願意付那筆利息錢，還有利息錢的利息，
更甭提物品折損後要花的錢。

Consider then, when you are tempted to buy any unnecessary Housholdstuff, or any superfluous thing, whether you will be willing to pay Interest, and Interest upon

Interest for it as long as you live; and more if it grows worse by using.

6

嫌貨才是買貨人。

He that speaks ill of the Mare, will buy her.

7

許多人因為買了好東西，從此受害無比。

Many have been ruin'd by buying good pennyworths.

8

買貨時，最好付現不賒帳，因為接受賒帳，會預期有百分之五的壞帳拿不回來，所以他會在貨品的標籤上，將預期的損失先加上。想挑願意賒帳交易的買家，就得支付這筆帳。付現若痛快，或許就能免掉這筆帳。

In buying Goods, 'tis best to pay ready Money, because, He that sells upon Credit, expects to lose 5 per Cent. by bad Debts: therefore he charges, on all he sells upon Credit, an Advance that shall make up that Deficiency. Those who pay for what they buy upon Credit, pay their Share of this Advance. He that pays ready Money, escapes or may escape that Charge.

9 要買東西，要有一百隻眼睛；要賣東西，只要一隻眼睛。
He who buys had need have 100 Eyes, but one's enough for him that sells the Stuff.

10 為人誠實又精打細算，一年雖只賺六英鎊，用處如同一百英鎊。天天都花上四便士，一年花掉超過六英鎊，代價相當於一百英鎊。（譯註：一英鎊相當於二百四十便士）
For 6 l. a Year, you may have the Use of 100 l. if you are a Man of known Prudence and Honesty.

窮理查說：

「買你不需要的東西，持續賣掉你的生活所需。」

1　一個窮字百樣缺。
For one poor Man there are an hundred indigent.

2　廚房太大間（編註：喻太注重享受），意志最不堅。
A fat kitchin, a lean Will.

3　嗜慾若多，再多的東西都不夠。

4 愛慕虛榮的確是種空虛的詛咒；你要是迷戀任何風潮，最好
先看看你的荷包。
Fond Pride of Dress is sure an empty Curse; E're Fancy you consult, consult your
Purse.

5 裙擺做得長，錢包輕得慌。
A large train makes a light Purse.

6 絲緞能滅廚房火。（編註：講究穿戴，就要小心勒緊褲袋餓肚子）
Silks and Sattins put out the Kitchen Fire.

7 富裕剛在馬背上坐好，韁繩就放掉，隨即就從鞍上被甩掉。

8 克制最初的慾望還不算難事，滿足隨之而來的其他慾望才最難辦。

'Tis easier to suppress the first Desire, than to satisfy all that follow it.

When Prosperity was well mounted, she let go the Bridle, and soon came tumbling out of the Saddle.

9 紅布、絲品和天鵝絨，都能滅了廚房爐火。

Scarlet, Silk and Velvet, have put out the Kitchen Fire.

10 美色與美酒，賭博與詐欺，會讓財富貶低，慾望無底。

Women & Wine, Game & Deceit, Make the Wealth small and the Wants great.

11 比起不讓一支煙囪熄火，蓋兩支煙囪要容易得多。

12 揮霍的人常比貪婪的人更不義。
The Prodigal generally does more Injustice than the Covetous.

13 痛飲眨眼三百杯，掏錢卻要找三天。
He that drinks fast, pays slow.

14 許多人都認為自己買到了享受，但其實是將自己賣給了享受當奴隸。
Many a Man thinks he is buying Pleasure, when he is really selling himself a Slave to it.

15 當水井乾涸，我們才知道水的價值幾何。

16 要是人能滿足一半願望，就會多出一倍的麻煩。
If Man could have Half his Wishes, he would double his Troubles.

17 花錢如流水，借錢爛債鬼。
Great spenders are bad lenders.

18 農夫站得挺，高過仕紳跪屈膝。
A Plowman on his Legs is higher than a Gentleman on his Knees.

窮理查說：

「不當信託、不要爭辯、不要作保、不要借錢，你就能終生平穩享天年。」

1 債主是迷信的一群人，凡事都要挑日子看時辰。

The Creditors are a superstitious sect, great observers of set days and times.

2 欠債的總比不上債主記性佳。

Creditors have better memories than debtors.

3 想要知道錢財的價值，去借一些你就知。

If you'd know the Value of Money, go and borrow some.

4 債務人是債主的奴隸；保人是雙方的奴隸。
The Borrower is a Slave to the Lender; the Security to both.

5 債務的身上，背負著「撒謊」。
Lying rides upon Debt's back.

6 付清你的債，你值多少自己就會明白。
Pay what you owe, and what you're worth you'll know.

7 有人向你短期借貸，借他時別忘了復活節時催還債。（編註：想拿回借出去的錢就像耶穌復活一樣難）
He that would have a short Lent, let him borrow Money to be repaid at Easter.

8 人走了，啥事都撒手，只記得跟他的債主道再見。

He's gone, and forgot nothing but to say Farewel——to his creditors.

9 寧可花錢買，不要去借貸。

Borgen macht sorgen.

10 借錢給敵人，能化敵為友；借錢給朋友，很快就沒朋友。

Lend Money to an Enemy, and thou'lt gain him, to a Friend and thou'lt lose him.

11 付清你所欠的，就知到底哪些才是你自己的。

Pay what you owe, and you'll know what's your own.

窮理查說：

「貪婪未曾見幸福，怎將兩者當一路。」

1 錢字擺中間，榮辱就會被放到兩邊。

Neither Shame nor Grace yet Bob.

2 有錢人，錢奴才。

He does not possess Wealth, it possesses him.

3 窮困會想要有東西，奢華要的是許多東西，貪婪要的是所有的東西。

Poverty wants some things, Luxury many things, Avarice all things.

4 窮人有點錢，乞丐啥都欠；富人賺到飽，貪婪仍無厭。

The Poor have little, Beggars none; the Rich too much, enough not one.

5 「貪婪」無所不用其極的累積，經常被「野心」愚蠢地揮霍殆盡。

Ambition often spends foolishly what Avarice had wickedly collected.

6 人如果有寬大的心田，最不在乎的就是錢，但可惜的是——絕大多數人，都只覺得缺錢。

The generous Mind least regards money, and yet most feels the Want of it.

7 即使其他罪過都已經垂垂老矣，貪婪還充滿了青春的活力，讓人在聖誕時節還貪無止期。

When other Sins grow old by Time, then Avarice is in its prime, yet feed the Poor at Christmas time.

8 狗眼看人低，將錢當印記，審判日時只剩你自己。

Fient de chien, & marc d'argent, Seront tout un au jour du jugement.

9 有錢買不通死神。

Death takes no bribes.

窮理查說：

「財富不在累積多，真能享受才快活。」

1 如果你的錢財屬於你，何不帶著一起歸西？
If your Riches are yours, why don't you take them with you to the t'other World?

2 小房子住得好，小田地耕耘好，家裡的老婆心地好，才是真正的富豪。
A little House well fill'd, a little Field well till'd, and a little Wife well will'd, are great Riches.

3 金錢加上良好舉止，才能塑造一個紳士。

4 認為金錢萬能，很容易被當成拜金的人。

He that is of Opinion Money will do every Thing, may well be suspected of doing every Thing for Money.

窮理查說：

「富人何需省儉，省儉何需當富人。」

1　聖誕大餐的飯禱要注意，別使餐桌成陷阱，要將上帝的恩澤分享給貧苦人民。

In Christmas Feasting pray take care; Let not your table be a Snare; but with the Poor God's Bounty Share.

2　祝小氣鬼長命百歲，實在是一點好處也沒。

Wish a miser long life, and you wish him no good.

3　有蘋果酒可喝卻獨酌，乾脆馬兒也讓你自己捉。

He that drinks his Cyder alone, let him catch his Horse alone.

4 關懷加倍，富裕加倍。
He who multiplies Riches multiplies Cares.

5 再怎麼樂善好施，也不會降低生活品質。
Great-Alms-giving, lessens no Man's Living.

6 為富不仁者，好比肥山豬，你要他付出，除非進棺木。
A rich rogue, is like a fat hog, who never does good til as dead as a log.

窮理查說：

「人若不滿足，沒一張椅子堪稱舒服。」

1 滿足與富裕，湊不在一起，富裕找上你，我要滿足就足矣。

Content and Riches seldom meet together, Riches take thou, contentment I had rather.

2 能知足，窮人也富有；不知足，富人也窮窘。

Content makes poor men rich; Discontent makes rich Men poor.

3 古代哲學家說過，幸福倚靠內在的氣質高低，勝過依賴外在的物質好壞；不能在任何狀況感到幸福的人，在任何狀況都沒法獲得幸福。要得到幸福，他們説，必定要能夠知足。沒錯！但是他們沒教我們怎樣才能知足。窮理查要為您提供一條簡便的原則：若想要知足，就轉頭看看那些財物比你少的人，別看著財物多過你的人。如果你這樣還不知足，你活該不幸福。

Some antient Philosophers have said, that Happiness depends more on the inward Disposition of Mind than on outward Circumstances; and that he who cannot be happy in any State, can be so in no State. To be happy, they tell us we must be content. But they do not teach how we may become content. Poor Richard shall give you a short good Rule for that. To be content, look backward on those who possess less than yourself, not forward on those who possess more. If this does not make you content, you don't deserve to be happy.

4 知足才是賢者之石的名，因為它能點石成金。

Content is the Philosopher's Stone, that turns all it touches into Gold.

5 滿足和富裕，並不總是一對好伴侶。

6

要求與擁有，有時真算是昂貴的買賣。

Ask and have, is sometimes dear buying.

part 2

窮理查教你比別人
更成功

可敬的讀者：

我盼望您的收穫同我一樣豐盈。因為除了星象預測以及其他年曆中通常會寫的內容，好提供來年日常所需以外，就沒有其他價值了，所以我不斷寫些道德格言、明智準則，與智慧語錄，有許多相當言簡意賅的好話，我打算給年輕人留下一些深刻而持久的印象，即便屆時這份年曆和年曆的作者早已不復存在他們記憶之中，也能讓他們終身受用。

如果我偶爾穿插一、兩則笑話，看起來沒有什麼用處，我得道個歉，因為它們也有它們的用處，因為漫不經心的人可能因為這些笑話而細心研讀，因而會被更重要的內容所影響。每個月開頭的詩句，大概也都是出自同樣的用意。我不用向您細述其中有多少是我自己的創作，要是您對這些詩句有任何判斷力，就能明白巧匠和拙手的差異了。

我跟您都知道，我不是天生的詩人；這是我從沒學過的技藝，我也實在學不會。要是我有什麼詩可作，一定是大自然和星座，讓我這麼做。既然別人的佳作這麼多，我又到底為什麼要讓讀者看到我自己的拙作？要是市場上有著許多好上十倍的菜色可買，卻把自耕自種的粗茶淡飯擺在客人面前，我覺得這對取悅客戶來說，實在是說不過去。相反地，我向您保證，朋友，我已經努力為您呈現最好的東西，而且對您大大有益。

──《窮理查年鑑》一七四七年

想想三件事：
你從何處來，
要往何處去，
應該看重誰。

窮理查說：

「什麼東西比黃金更有價值？鑽石。比鑽石更有價值的是什麼？品德。」

1 草本植物裡，有好處的多；在人類之中，有品德的少。

Much Virtue in Herbs, little in Men.

2 豬要肥美，人要德美。

The excellency of hogs is fatness, of men virtue.

3 做人缺德沒品行，好比一身破爛。

He is ill cloth'd, who is bare of Virtue.

4 有愛缺義氣，有義沒權力，有權沒志氣，立志欠努力，努力沒收益，獲利少德性，全都是個屁。

Relation without friendship, friendship without power, power without will, will witho. effect, effect without profit, & profit without vertue, are not worth a farto.

5 極端的美貌、極度的力量、極多的財富，卻都真的沒有極大用處；一副正直的心腸就勝過它們全部。

Great Beauty, great strength, & great Riches, are really & truly of no great Use; a right Heart exceeds all.

6 沒德行就沒自由；這道律則對個人和公眾都適用。

No longer virtuous no longer free; is a Maxim as true with regard to a private Person as a Common-wealth.

7 美德不一定能讓長相好看，惡行卻一定會讓面目難看。

Virtue may not always make a Face handsome, but Vice will certainly make it ugly.

8 若是能有德，會比國王還快樂。

You may be more happy than Princes, if you will be more virtuous.

9 美德為母，女兒就是幸福。

Virtue and Happiness are Mother and Daughter.

10 遵循德性，常保德性，其他萬事，聽天由命。

Seek Virtue, and, of that possest, To Providence, resign the rest.

11 人若沒禮貌，品德就顯更需要。

A Man without ceremony has need of great merit in its place.

12 學好人或裝好人，大有不同該區分。

There is much difference between imitating a good man, and counterfeiting him.

13 沒人能夠無德卻有福。

Beatus esse sine Virtute, nemo potest.

歐巴馬（美國前總統）

班傑明・富蘭克林最早在《窮理查年鑑》中推廣的所有那些樸實的美德，持續鼓舞著一代又一代人盡忠於我們的國家。這些美德分別是：自力更生、自我提升和敢於冒險的價值觀；自我激勵、自律自制和努力工作的價值觀；節儉和勇於承擔個人責任的價值觀。

窮理查說：

「能夠獲得榮耀的捷徑，就是做事全靠良心。」

1 良知是人都需要，但少數人才當寶，沒人覺得自己有缺少。

Good Sense is a Thing all need, few have, and none think they want.

2 罪惡不是因為本身遭禁止而令人痛苦，它遭受禁止是因為令人痛苦。責任也不是因為本身被要求才對人有益，它被要求是因為對人有益。

Sin is not hurtful because it is forbidden but it is forbidden because it's hurtful. Nor is a Duty beneficial because it is commanded, but it is commanded, because it's beneficial.

3 沒有事物比「良善」更受大家喜歡。
Nothing so popular as GOODNESS.

4 沒有什麼物品，能比良善更有價值。
A Man has no more Goods than he gets Good by.

5 敢將棘刺四處撒，最好不要赤足走天下。
He that scatters Thorns, let him not go barefoot.

6 做了你不該做的，就會聽到你不想聽的。
If you do what you should not, you must hear what you would not.

7 不該做的事卻去做，就會有不想要的感受。
He that doth what he should not, shall feel what he would not.

8 君子坦蕩蕩，小人常戚戚。

A good Man is seldom uneasy, an ill one never easie.

9 不敢做壞事，就不用害怕任何事。

Fear to do ill, and you need fear nought else.

10 你要是傷害良心，良心不會放過你。

If thou injurest Conscience, it will have its Revenge on thee.

11 良心常保清白，恐懼從此不來。

Keep Conscience clear, Then never fear.

12 你若想要過得安心，就做你該做的，而不是自己討開心。

Would you live with ease, Do what you ought, and not what you please.

13 清白又無辜，才是法庭上的最佳辯護。

Innocence is its own Defence.

14 要是做壞事，歡樂就消逝，苦痛一點也沒消失；如果做好事，痛苦會消逝，歡樂卻能一直維持。

If thou dost ill, the joy fades, not the pains. If well, the pain doth fade, the joy remains.

15 有些人學了太多而發瘋，但沒人學著行善而發瘋。

Some men grow mad by studying much to know. But who grows mad by studying good to grow.

16 要行得正當，要嚴斥誹謗；塵土上得了泥牆，卻不能對大理石有一絲損傷。

Act uprightly, and despise Calumny; Dirt may stick to a Mud Wall, but not to polish'd Marble.

17 讓先人受評斷時是依他們自己所長，讓我們受評斷時是看我們自己有多善良。

Let our Fathers and Grandfathers be valued for their Goodness, ourselves for our own.

18 你的心腸要和你的地位權力成正比，否則上帝就要按你的心腸來排定你的階級。

Proportion your Charity to the Strength of your Estate, or God will proportion your Estate to the Weakness of your Charity.

19 承受傷害多，比傷人好過。

It is better to take many Injuries than to give one.

20 行善莫推遲；別像聖喬治，雖然是騎士，上馬卻是沒半次。

Defer not thy well-doing; be not like St. George, who is always a horseback, and never rides on.

21 世上最尊貴的問題，就是：「我這麼做能成就什麼善？」
The noblest question in the world is What Good may I do in it?

22 不窺視他人信件、不竊取他人財物、不探聽他人祕密。
Nor Eye in a letter, nor Hand in a purse, nor Ear in the secret of another.

23 惡行知道自己醜，所以會拿面具蓋住頭。
Vice knows she's ugly, so puts on her Mask.

24 好好過活，才能讓你長命；因為愚笨跟邪惡都要人短命。
If thou wouldst live long, live well; for Folly and Wickedness shorten Life.

25 用什麼來服侍神？行好事，做好人。
What is Serving God? 'Tis doing Good to Man.

26 良心雖安靜，能在雷下睡，安心和內疚，彼此相隔千萬里。

A quiet Conscience sleeps in Thunder, but Rest and Guilt live far asunder.

27 善良的閃亮根源！快快降臨我的身邊，看守我的內心，注意我的語言。

Bright Source of Goodness! to my Aid descend.Watch o'er my Heart, and all my Words attend.

28 缺德的英雄，不敢面對清白的凡人。

A wicked Hero will turn his back to an innocent coward.

29 家中窗戶若是玻璃做，就不要向鄰戶砸石頭。（編註：傷人小心惹來報復）

Don't throw stones at your neighbours, if your own windows are glass.

窮理查說：「偉人能謙卑，尊崇變兩倍。」

1 「成功」毀了不少人。

Success has ruin'd many a Man.

2 人家說「驕傲」是好人最難根除的惡習。它是個變形蟲，以各種面貌掩藏自己，有時候甚至會戴上謙卑的面具。如果有人對打扮得整潔得體感到驕傲，也會有其他人對此鄙夷，總是意興闌珊。

PRIDE is said to be the last vice the good man gets clear of. 'Tis a meer Proteus, and disguises itself under all manner of appearances, putting on sometimes even the mask of humility. If some are proud of neatness and propriety of dress; others are equally so of despising it, and acting the perpetual sloven.

3 驕傲自誇還得意洋洋！膨風的巴佛趾高氣昂，好比一隻癩蛤蟆，還沒有其他蛤蟆在身旁。

Mark with what insolence and pride, Blown Bufo takes his haughty stride; As if no toad was toad beside.

4 驕傲的人也討厭別人的驕傲。

The Proud hate Pride—in others.

5 我們可以挑別人的毛病，抱怨灰塵遮了他們的眼睛，一點瑕疵缺陷都不放過，卻看不到自己更大的過錯。

In other men we faults can spy, And blame the mote that dims their eye; Each little speck and blemish find: To our own stronger errors blind.

6 傲慢與卑鄙，關係當然匪淺，就算藕斷絲也連。

Great Pride and Meanness sure are near ally'd; Or thin Partitions do their Bounds divide.

7 驕傲跟欠缺都是大聲嚷嚷的乞丐，但是驕傲比起欠缺還要更無賴。

Pride is as loud a Beggar as Want, and a great deal more saucy.

8 第一等蠢事，是自以為英明睿智；第二等蠢事，是宣稱如此；第三等蠢事，是對所有勸告都鄙視。

The first Degree of Folly, is to conceit one's self wise; the second to profess it; the third to despise Counsel.

9 絕望只會讓某些人受傷，傲慢卻害許多人遭殃。

Despair ruins some, Presumption many.

10 對上級謙卑是責任，對平輩謙卑是禮貌學問，對弱者謙卑則是高尚人。

To be humble to Superiors is Duty, to Equals Courtesy, to Inferiors Nobleness.

11 驕傲要果腹，吃的就是輕蔑與虛榮。
Pride dines upon Vanity, sups on Contempt.

12 驕傲上了馬車，羞恥跟著上車。
Pride gets into the Coach, and Shame mounts behind.

13 驕傲若要做前鋒，赤貧便會當後衛。
If Pride leads the Van, Beggary brings up the Rear.

14 驕傲一抬頭，幸福躡步走。
As Pride increases, Fortune declines.

15 信心過了頭，才會被騙成了冤大頭。
None are deceived but they that confide.

16
別高估自己的小聰明，忘了別人的機警：一個精明的人，會輸給一個精明人加上半個精明人。

Don't think so much of your own Cunning, as to forget other Mens: A cunning Man is overmatch'd by a cunning Man and a Half.

17
不要自誇你所知，不要自滿你所持，不要自負你所有，不要自矜你所能。

Proclaim not all thou knowest, all thou owest, all thou hast, nor all thou canst.

18
無名小卒與謙卑，讓其他人物與德行的價值翻十倍。

A Cypher and Humility make the other Figures & Virtues of ten-fold Value.

19
為知識驕傲，是盯著光源看到眼睛瞎掉；為品德驕傲，是拿著解毒劑給自己下毒藥。

To be proud of Knowledge, is to be blind with Light; to be proud of Virtue, is to poison yourself with the Antidote.

20
有了學問與聰明，還得學會智慧與謙虛。
If thou hast wit & learning, add to it Wisdom and Modesty.

21
害羞這項品德好，就跟驕傲一樣妙。
Great Merit is coy, as well as great Pride.

22
崎嶇地面最容易磨破皮，驕傲的人最容易受人抨擊。
As sore places meet most rubs, proud folks meet most affronts.

23
對自己的主張，小有不安總好過自滿張狂。
Better is a little with content than much with contention.

24
謙遜是美德，害羞卻是惡。
Tho', Modesty is a Virtue, Bashfulness is a Vice.

25 傲慢先讓人盲目，再讓人忙碌。

Presumption first blinds a Man, then sets him a running.

26 登高必自卑。

In success be moderate.

27 自負比壞心更中傷人。

Vanity backbites more than Malice.

28 對驕傲嗆聲，並不總是謙卑的象徵。

Declaiming against Pride, is not always a Sign of Humility.

29 過度的謙恭，往往會掩蓋最棒的德行。

Great Modesty often hides great Merit.

30

痛風與驕恣，很難徹底醫治。

Pride and the Gout, are seldom cur'd throughout.

31

謙虛明智者最有福，位高權重也會沉淪，低微卑下也能突出；無恥者自作踐，自作自受沒人憐。

In prosperous fortunes be modest and wise, the greatest may fall, and the lowest may rise: but insolent People that fall in disgrace, are wretched and no-body pities their Case.

32

卑賤是傲慢的原因。

Meanness is the Parent of Insolence.

查理·蒙格

我可以告訴你很多關於沃倫（指巴菲特）的事，像他老是提醒我班傑明·富蘭克林的事；所以，我也可以告訴你很多關於班傑明·富蘭克林的事。

窮理查說：「誠實的人先苦後樂；地痞流氓總是先樂後苦。」

1 編造一定得付錢打點，真相卻能赤裸呈現。

Craft must be at charge for clothes, but Truth can go naked.

2 這種事兒人常有：編六個藉口，代替一個真理由。

It's common for Men to give 6 pretended Reasons instead of one real one.

3 一個公開的偽君子就不可能完成任何具影響力的大事。因為他不能夠得到人們的信任，也就不能得到他們的協助，所以只剩下他自己靠自己的屁股；就算是在他自己活動的領域裡，他能做的也都只會遭人鄙棄。

A discovered Dissembler can atchieve nothing great or considerable. For not being able to gain Mens Trust, he cannot gain their Concurrence; and so is left alone to act singly and upon his own Bottom; and while that is the Sphere of his Activity, all that he can do must needs be contemptible.

4 不刺探祕密是睿智，不揭露祕密是誠實。

It is wise not to seek a Secret, and Honest not to reveal it.

5 謊言只靠獨腳撐，實話兩腳站得穩。

A Lie stands on 1 leg, Truth on 2.

6 承諾會為你爭取到朋友，但失信會將這些朋友變成寇讎。

Promises may get thee Friends, but Nonperformance will turn them into Enemies.

7 搞計謀、耍花招，都是傻子的做法，因為他們還沒聰明到當個誠實佬。

Tricks and Treachery are the Practice of Fools, that have not Wit enough to be honest.

8 撒謊堪稱第二壞——最糟糕的是躲債。

The second Vice is Lying; the first is Running in Debt.

9 筆下惡意多過事實，會讓作家墮落成登徒子。

When there's more Malice shown than Matter; on the Writer falls the satyr.

10 看起來光像沒用處，得要成真才算數。（編註：做人要坦誠、說到做到——說你所擁有的，履行你的承諾）

What you would seem to be, be really.

窮理查說：

「勤勉有耐心，老鼠咬斷粗鋼筋。」

1 少說，多做。
Speak little, do much.

2 良言不如善行。
Well done is better than well said.

3 工作要像能活一百歲那樣認真，禱告得像明天就要死了那樣虔誠。
Work as if you were to live 100 Years. Pray as if you were to die To-morrow.

4 懶惰又沉默，傻人當美德。
Sloth and Silence are a Fool's Virtues.

5 愈愛唱高調，愈是辦不到。
Great Talkers, little Doers.

6 只要工夫下得深，小刀鋸斷老樹根。
Little Strokes, Fell great Oaks.

7 努力為幸運之母。
Diligence is the Mother of Good-Luck.

8 勤奮者知道，天下無難事；怠惰者只知，事事全難事。
All things are easy to Industry, All things difficult to Sloth.

9 不拼到死，不會留名青史。（編註：吃得苦中苦，方為人上人）

No man e'er was glorious, who was not laborious.

10 有恆者，事竟成。

He that can have Patience, can have what he will.

11 不要成天想投機，上帝就不會讓你下地獄。

Keep thou from the Opportunity, and God will keep thee from the Sin.

12 將自己家族當成榮耀真丟臉！你該為自己家族爭臉面。

'Tis a Shame that your Family is an Honour to you! You ought to be an Honour to your Family.

窮理查說：

「只會縱慾荒淫的人，別妄想千古留姓名。」

1 惡化的傷口還能治，惡化的名聲沒藥醫。

An ill Wound, but not an ill Name, may be healed.

2 玻璃、瓷器和名譽，脆弱易碎，修補不易。

Glass, China, and Reputation, are easily crack'd, and never well mended.

3 野狼偶爾飽餐綿羊一兩隻，人們動輒吞下上萬隻。

A wolf eats sheep but now and then, Ten Thousands are devour'd by Men.

4 美酒、佳餚、美女、懶散，都要有節制，不然痛風會纏著你到死。

Be temperate in wine, in eating, girls, & sloth; Or the Gout will seize you and plague you both.

5 沒有什麼比過度的快樂更痛苦，也沒有什麼比過多的自由（或放縱）更令人感到束縛。

Nothing brings more pain than too much pleasure; nothing more bondage than too much liberty, (or libertinism).

窮理查說：

「天助自助者。」

1 在凱撒心裡，凱旋戰車不足奇，戰勝自己才得意。
Caesar did not merit the triumphal Car, more than he that conquers himself.

2 閱讀會讓人更豐富，沉思能夠令人有深度，討論則使人思路更清楚。
Reading makes a full Man, Meditation a profound Man, discourse a clear Man.

3 要活用你的天賦，不用鑽子來督促。
You may drive a gift without a gimblet.

4 別把你的天分掩蓋住，它們天生有用處。

Hide not your Talents, they for Use were made.

5 曠世天才自己的王國裡住，好比金礦藏深處。

A fine genius in his own country, is like gold in the mine.

6 無知還不算可恥，不願學習才丟臉。

Being ignorant is not so much a Shame, as being unwilling to learn.

7 向前看，免得落後一大群。

Look before, or you'll find yourself behind.

8 多學學巧匠這一手：凡事靠自修，師傅還當他是笨頭。

Learn of the skilful: He that teaches himself, hath a fool for his master.

9 **日晷放在陰影裡，這是什麼玩意！**（編註：放在陰影裡的日晷沒用處，做人要好好發揮自己的才能）

What's a Sun-Dial in the Shade!

10 **狡詐多計，主要來自沒能力。**

Cunning proceeds from Want of Capacity.

窮理查說：

「說得愈多，錯愈多。」

1 許多人的嘴，證明了他們自己多麼沒智慧。
Many a Man's own Tongue gives Evidence against his Understanding.

2 沉默並非總是智慧的標記，絮叨卻永遠都是愚蠢的象徵。
Silence is not always a Sign of Wisdom, but Babbling is ever a Mark of Folly.

3 失足復原快，失言麻煩甩不開。
A Slip of the Foot you may soon recover: But a Slip of the Tongue you may never get over.

4 想要一生平安順遂，別把一切所知都拿來說嘴，也別把一切所見都當成絕對。

He that would live in peace & at ease, Must not speak all he knows, nor judge all he sees.

5 自己的舌頭都管不住，怎能盼望拿「他人嚼舌根」有法度？

Since I cannot govern my own tongue, tho' within my own teeth, how can I hope to govern the tongues of others?

6 若將祕密對人講，你的自由就賣光。

To whom thy secret thou dost tell. To him thy freedom thou dost sell.

7 人的舌頭軟溜溜，裡面沒骨頭；可是話兒一出口，卻能折斷人家的骨頭。

Man's tongue is soft, and bone doth lack; Yet a stroke therewith may break a man's back.

8 失足好過失言。
Better slip with foot than tongue.

9 謹慎之人罕開口，八卦當做祕密守。
In a discreet man's mouth, a publick thing is private.

10 舌根莫亂嚼，大禍從口出。
Tongue double, brings trouble.

11 舌頭無骨，傷人入骨。
A soft Tongue may strike hard.

12 不當的讚辭，是苛刻的諷刺。
Praise to the undeserving, is severe Satyr.

13 舌頭說錯話，臉頰吃耳光。
The Tongue offends, and the Ears get the Cuffing.

14 長話要短說：緊閉的嘴巴鑽不進一隻蒼蠅。
Speak and speed; the close mouth catches no flies.

15 報復字詞雖少數，字詞卻常引報復。
There's small Revenge in Words, but Words may be greatly revenged.

16 笨頭偏愛賣弄口舌。
Half Wits talk much but say little.

17 長舌的人都該把耳朵剪掉，因為他們根本不需要。
Great talkers should be cropt, for they've no need of ears.

18 不想讓敵人知道什麼祕密，千萬別對朋友提起。
If you would keep your Secret from an enemy, tell it not to a friend.

19 別聽信朋友的閒話，也別說敵人的壞話。
Hear no ill of a Friend, nor speak any of an Enemy.

20 要傻瓜閉嘴很粗野，讓傻瓜講話很殘酷。
It is Ill-Manners to silence a Fool, and Cruelty to let him go on.

21 一知半解的哈利，什麼事情都能吹噓。
Harry Smatter, has a Mouth for every Matter.

22 傳道最勤屬螞蟻，口中從不說一語。（編註：身教勝於言傳）
None preaches better than the ant, and she says nothing.

23

全天下最好的事兒，就是舌頭受控制；說得太多，必定是話兒沒用。

Best is the Tongue that feels the rein; He that talks much, must talk in vain.

24

對一個吝嗇鬼說他有錢，對一個女人說她上了年紀，你既拿不到一毛錢，也見不到好脾氣。

Tell a miser he's rich, and a woman she's old, you'll get no money of one, nor kindness of t' other.

窮理查說：

「謹記窮理查一句話，憤怒行事總會惹笑話。」

1 憤怒從來不會沒理由，只是很少會是好理由。

Anger is never without a Reason, but seldom with a good One.

2 憤怒能讓東西溫暖，卻會燒壞鍋爐。

Anger warms the Invention, but overheats the Oven.

3 憤怒愚昧並肩走，怨恨緊跟在後頭。

4 為了他人使你失望而生氣？切記你可沒法一切靠自己。

Are you angry that others disappoint you? remember you cannot depend upon yourself.

5 忽視能夠消除傷害，報復卻會增加傷害。

Neglect kills Injuries. Revenge increases them.

6 誰若愛吵架，絕無好鄰家。

A quarrelsome Man has no good Neighbours.

7 把你的不滿當祕密；要是傳出去，全世界都要鄙視你，而且你會因此更不滿意。

8 人若激動，就像騎著的馬兒發了瘋。

A Man in a Passion rides a mad Horse.

窮理查說：

「一惡之不除，萬惡接連出。」

1 新的真理是真理，舊的過錯還是錯，只是笨蛋不會分。

A new truth is a truth, an old error is an error. Tho' Clodpate wont allow either.

2 文過飾非的痛苦，多過要人自己去彌補。

Men take more pains to mask than mend.

3 許多國王都犯了和大衛王同樣的罪，卻沒有多少人和他一樣懺悔。

Many Princes sin with David, but few repent with him.

4 決心今後要改過，就是決心不改眼前錯。

He that resolves to mend hereafter, resolves not to mend now.

5 今後悔改的決心，沒有一個是真心。

No Resolution of Repenting hereafter, can be sincere.

6 忽略小錯不彌補，隨即變成大錯誤。

Neglect mending a small Fault, and 'twill soon be a great One.

7 犯錯是人性，悔過是神性，執迷不悟是惡魔脾性。

To err is human, to repent divine, to persist devilish.

8 改正一個錯，相當於發現兩個錯，但發現一個錯，卻又好過犯兩個錯。

One Mend-fault is worth two Findfaults, but one Findfault is better than two Makefaults.

9 好人才懂得怎麼懺悔，好人才知道自己行止有虧。

None but the well-bred man knows how to confess a fault, or acknowledge himself in an error.

10 能夠忍受責難，而且改過遷善，這樣的人如果不是智者，就是在成為智者的康莊大道上。

He that can bear a Reproof, and mend by it, if he is not wise, is in a fair way of being so.

11 勇於面對自己錯誤，或是有決心改正自己錯誤的人，實在是太少了！

How few there are who have courage enough to own their Faults, or resolution enough to mend them!

12　小錯得過且過；大過就得牢記心頭。
Wink at small faults; remember thou hast great ones.

13　有勇有智，才敢自承做錯事。
The Wise and Brave dares own that he was wrong.

14　偷兒雖小，容易變成大盜。
Little Rogues easily become great Ones.

窮理查說：

「每年根除一個壞習慣，惡棍遲早也能變好漢。」

1 野狼每年都換毛，但牠習性永遠改不了。

The Wolf sheds his Coat once a Year, his Disposition never.

2 注意他人的優點，當心自己的缺陷。

Search others for their virtues, thy self for thy vices.

3 避免養成壞習慣，比不上根除惡習難。

4 什麼樣叫強？把自己惡習改光光。什麼樣叫富？對自己所有能感到滿足。

Who is strong? He that can conquer his bad Habits. Who is rich? He that rejoices in his Portion.

5 過年換掉舊年曆，順便擺脫舊惡習，雖然也曾那麼親密。

With the old Almanack and the old Year, Leave thy old Vices, tho' ever so dear.

6 別讓壞習慣活得比你長。

Let thy vices die before thee.

窮理查說：

「聽不進建議，沒人能幫你。」

1 智者從敵人那得到的收穫，比傻瓜從朋友那得來的更多。

The wise Man draws more Advantage from his Enemies, than the Fool from his Friends.

2 經驗是間好學校，但是傻瓜不會再上其他的學校。

Experience keeps a dear school, yet Fools will learn in no other.

3 從別人的危險中得到警告，真是有福報。

Felix quem faciunt aliena pericula cautum.

4 好的例子，是最好的啟示。

A good Example is the best sermon.

5 一盎司買到的智慧，值過一磅學來的教訓。

An ounce of wit that is bought, Is worth a pound that is taught.

6 不懂聽令，不會號令。（編註：先跟隨有經驗的人學習，才會知道如何領導）

He that cannot obey, cannot command.

7 我們能夠提供建議，卻不能幫人處理。（編註：喻規劃執行終究得靠自己）

We may give Advice, but we cannot give Conduct.

8 傻瓜什麼建議都需要，但智者只要其中好的那幾條。

Fools need Advice most, but wise Men only are the better for it.

9
啊，笨頭笨腦！年紀還小，就有了兩個寶，時間和忠告；只是一個你弄丟，另一個卻又不要。

Ah simple Man! when a boy two precious jewels were given thee, Time, and good Advice: one thou hast lost, and the other thrown away.

10
智者從他人受的傷害當中學習；傻子從自己所受的傷害中得教訓。

Wise Men learn by others harms: Fools by their own.

查理‧蒙格來自富蘭克林的《窮理查年鑑》：「**一盎司買到的智慧，值過一磅學來的教訓。**」富蘭克林這句話的部分含義是，為了避免發生「不一致傾向」，預防習慣的養成，要比改變習慣容易得多。

窮理查說：

「耐心要怎麼衡量？就看你找尋東西的模樣。」

1 做事不要怕太晚，但也別衝太快。
Be not sick too late, nor well too soon.

2 急事緩辦。
Make haste slowly.

3 沒摸清門道，別妄動手腳。

Do not do that which you would not have known.

4 後見之明易，先見之明難。
Tis easy to see, hard to foresee.

5 重要時刻，要能自我克制。
At a great Pennyworth, pause a while.

6 急匆匆，少建功。
Eilen thut selten gut.

7 欲速則不達。
Haste makes Waste.

窮理查說：

「理性在講道理時，要是不聽，打你老大耳括子。」

1 聽從理性，不然道理也會壓過你。

Hear Reason, or she'll make you feel her.

2 理智一短少，什麼都想要。

Where Sense is wanting, every thing is wanting.

3 控制激情就是主人，服從激情就是僕人。

He is a Governor that governs his Passions, and he a Servant that serves them.

4 尼克的激情發得快又猛；他的理智看來卻像是一場空！

Nick's Passions grow fat and hearty; his Understanding looks consumptive!

5 激情若要衝刺，要讓理性控制。

If Passion drives, let Reason hold the Reins.

6 激情之止，懺悔之始。

The end of Passion is the beginning of Repentance.

秘訣 15

窮理查說：

「當覺得自己正確無誤的時候，你很可能錯得離譜。」

1 最堅硬的東西有三種：鋼鐵、鑽石和自知。

There are three Things extreamly hard, Steel, a Diamond and to know one's self.

2 除了你自己，還有誰更常騙你？

Who has deceiv'd thee so oft as thy self?

3 傻子笨得藏不住自己的智慧有多少。

克里斯·查布利斯 & 丹尼爾·西蒙斯

（心理學搞笑諾貝爾獎得主，主導心理學上最著名的實驗之一「看不見的大猩猩」）

「最堅硬的東西有三種：鋼鐵、鑽石和自知。」……我們需要被提醒不要被外表矇騙，因為我們傾向把外觀表象視為內在品質的確實呈現。我們需要被告誡，省一毛錢就等於多賺一毛錢，因為我們會差別看待「賺進來的錢」與「已經擁有的錢」。這些警世格言都是為了幫助我們避開直覺造成的錯誤而存在。

同樣的，富蘭克林所指稱的世間最堅硬、困難的東西，也暗示了對於「我們很了解自己」這樣的直覺信念應該加以質疑。在行經的人生之路上，我們好像非常了解自己的心智運作與行

窮理查年鑑

140

He's a Fool that cannot conceal his Wisdom.

為背後的成因，但事實上，很多時候我們根本毫無頭緒。

4 許多人都抱怨自己的記憶不行，卻很少有人抱怨自己的判斷不清。
Many complain of their Memory, few of their Judgment.

5 世上何事最容易？自己騙自己。
It's the easiest Thing in the World for a Man to deceive himself.

6 人人都自認，自己是好人。
All Mankind are beholden to him that is kind to the Good.

7 不幸的人沒人認識，幸運兒自己卻不知。
None know the unfortunate, and the fortunate do not know themselves.

8 大多數的傻子，都覺得自己只是無知。

Most Fools think they are only ignorant.

9 誰對一個人的判斷最準？是他自己還是他的敵人？

Who judges best of a Man, his Enemies or himself?

10 火爆湯姆真走運，看不見自己駝背的情形。

Happy Tom Crump, ne'er sees his own Hump.

窮理查說：

「虛榮開得了花，但結不了果。」

1 好好裝潢你的房子，別用你的房子來裝飾你。

Grace thou thy House, and let not that grace thee.

2 飽肚鼓鼓，罪惡之母。（編註：貪婪是罪惡根源）

A full Belly is the Mother of all Evil.

3 湯姆，虛榮會使你苦痛難挨；這些註定要失敗：豬尾巴做不出好箭來。

Tom, vain's your Pains; They all will fail: Ne'er was good Arrow made of a Sow's Tail.

4 別從人們週日的裝束衡量他們的虔誠和財富。

Don't judge of Mens Wealth or Piety, by their Sunday Appearances.

5 蝴蝶是什麼？頂多是隻毛蟲打扮過。

What is a butterfly? At best He's but a caterpiller drest.

窮理查說：

「要成人中豪傑，就靠意志堅決。」

1 三月風，四月雨，才能讓五月更顯得萬人迷。

March windy, and April rainy, makes May the pleasantest month of any.

2 歷經苦難和損失，會使人變得謙卑睿智。

After crosses and losses, men grow humbler & wiser.

3 要有偉大的決心很容易，難的是認真做下去。

Tis easy to frame a good bold resolution; but hard is the Task that concerns execution.

4 沒有沒樹皮的木頭。（編註：樹皮總粗糙，要取得木材得先經一番修整）

No Wood without Bark.

5 難題總求審慎解。

Weighty Questions ask for deliberate Answers.

6 令人受傷的事會讓人得到啟示。

The Things which hurt, instruct.

7 為了自己，否定自己。（編註：適當的約束自己是為了自己好）

Deny self for self's sake.

窮理查說：

「太陽從不悔過，也從不要求報酬。」

1 一無所求的人有福氣，因為他永遠不會失望和喪氣。

Blessed is he that expects nothing, for he shall never be disappointed.

2 換床治癒不了熱病，換工作也治癒不了不滿的心靈。

Discontented Minds, and Fevers of the Body are not to be cured by changing Beds or Businesses.

3 對於快樂能放手，快樂自然跟你走。

Fly Pleasures, and they'll follow you.

窮理查說：

「勿傻，勿精，但要智慧能分明。」

1 二十歲時，意志作主；三十歲時，機智作主；四十歲時，判斷作主。

At 20 years of age the Will reigns; at 30 the Wit; at 40 the Judgment.

2 常言道，智者只聽半套。

Le sage entend a demi mot.

3 天下沒有受騙的人，只是有人信以為真。

There's none deceived but he that trusts.

4
最善良的天性，沒有明智的指引，會變成最大的不幸。

Great Good-nature, without Prudence, is a great Misfortune.

5
說大話的人可能不是傻子，但相信他的人就絕對會是。

A great Talker may be no Fool, but he is one that relies on him.

6
傻瓜什麼建議都需要，但智者只要其中好的那幾條。

Fools need Advice most, but wise Men only are the better for it.

7
寒冷以及機靈，一樣都來自北地，但是，若只有機靈而沒有智慧，那就根本不值得一提。

Cold & cunning come from the north : but cunning sans coisdom is nothing worth.

8
魔鬼會將毒藥摻蜜水。

The Devil sweetens Poison with Honey.

9 如果夠聰明，就懂得小心；該怎麼對待別人的宗教、信用和眼睛。

You will be careful, if you are wise: How you touch Men's Religion, or Credit, or Eyes..

窮理查說……

「如果壞事不來，恐懼就是白費；壞事如果真的來，恐懼會讓痛苦加倍。」

1 享受現在時刻，留心過去時光；對於逐漸逼近的未來，不要恐懼也毋需盼望。

Enjoy the present hour, be mindful of the past; and neither fear nor wish the Approaches of the last.

2 貓兒腳上穿襪套，一隻老鼠也捉不到。

（編註：太過小心翼翼，就不容易成功，鼓勵人要積極一點）

The Cat in Gloves catches no Mice.

窮理查說：「人若安心無慮，恐怕安全堪虞。」

1 猜疑為防護之父，謹慎是安全之母。（編註：小心駛得萬年船）

Distrust & caution are the parents of security.

2 要讓自己廣為人知，但別讓人對你徹底熟知：看到淺灘的人定會隨意涉水過！

Let all Men know thee, but no man know thee thoroughly: Men freely ford that see the shallows.

3 有關公眾事務的第一個錯誤，就是盲目進入。

The first Mistake in publick Business, is the going into it.

4 要愛你的鄰居，但是別拆了你的圍籬。（編註：喻防人之心不可無）

Love your Neighbour; yet don't pull down your Hedge.

5 莫看天色雖然清，大衣帶著隨身行。（編註：未雨綢繆，做事要提前做準備）

When 'tis fair be sure take your Great coat with you.

6 嚐著甜頭，記著苦頭。（編註：居安思危）

When you taste Honey, remember Gall.

part 3

窮理查教你搞定
人脈好辦事

可敬的讀者：

除了查詢月份日期、重要日子、月相變化、日出月落時刻、潮汐與天氣的預測，就算我的年曆沒有其他好處，我想我的年曆還是值得你花錢買一本；因為我每年不斷為您準備這些內容與其他的天文趣事，至今已經將近木星的兩次公轉週期了。

但我希望您的收穫不只這些；因為為了提升您的心靈與地位，我不斷在各處添進一些道德訓示、智慧格言和行為準則，想要使您得到誠實、莊重、勤奮與節儉的好處；您如果確實採行，您的智慧與財富極有可能已經比買我這本年曆所花的錢多上好幾倍了。

——《窮理查年鑑》一七五六年

有人這麼說，該有的價值就是知
道朋友的價值為何；該有的美德
就是擁有敵人的美德。

一個人受大眾信任，不是由於他
自身，而是來自於眾人。

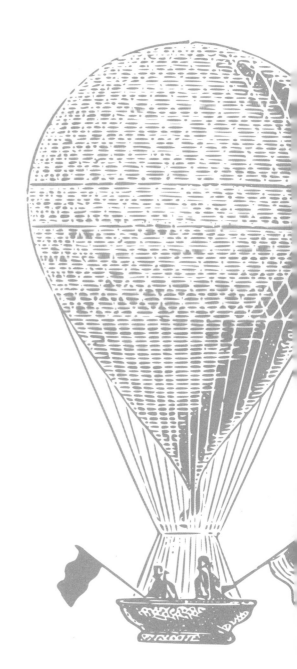

窮理查說：

「真正的友伴，是最好的財產。」

1 兄弟不一定是朋友，朋友卻永遠是弟兄。

A Brother may not be a Friend, but a Friend will always be a Brother.

2 維繫友誼不能靠客氣，更不能缺禮儀。

Friendship cannot live with Ceremony, nor without Civility.

3 公開的敵人大概是種詛咒，但是再怎麼樣也糟糕不過虛假的朋友。

An open Foe may prove a curse; But a pretended friend is worse.

4 要能尊敬所有人；要能服務多數人；要熟識少數人；當摯友要忠於一人；不要樹立敵人。

Be civil to all; serviceable to many; familiar with few; Friend to one; Enemy to none.

5 你無法戲弄敵人當你朋友；但你可以戲弄朋友成為敵人。

Thou canst not joke an Enemy into a Friend; but thou may'st a Friend into an Enemy.

6 人際關係最極致，是朋友明智而信實。

No better relation than a prudent & faithful Friend.

7 寧可多跟希臘的哲學家吃鹽，少跟義大利的弄臣吃那些蜜語甜言。

Thou hadst better eat salt with the Philosophers of Greece, than sugar with the Courtiers of Italy.

8 和狗一起躺下來，起來時跳蚤就會爬滿背。
He that lies down with Dogs, shall rise up with fleas.

9 想跟壞蛋打交道，名譽利益都不保。
There is neither honour nor gain, got in dealing with a villain.

10 跟愚笨的朋友太親密，就像帶著剃刀陪你上床去。
To be intimate with a foolish Friend, is like going to bed to a Razor.

11 虛偽的朋友與陰影，只在光芒耀眼時現形。
A false Friend and a Shadow, attend only while the Sun shines.

12 壞朋友，像條狗，就愛塵土起風波，愈髒愈快活。
Ill Company is like a dog who dirts those most, that he loves best.

13 挑朋友要慢，要比換朋友更慢。

Be slow in chusing a Friend, slower in changing.

14 朋友是王公貴族最怕的真幽靈。

Friends are the true Sceptres of Princes.

窮理查說：

「對其他人好，就是對自己最好。」

1 去愛，就被愛。
Love, and be lov'd.

2 若是想要訪客給笑臉，自己笑臉掛在先，至少看來也要有迎人笑面。
If you wou'd have Guests merry with your cheer, Be so your self, or so at least appear.

3 施恩慎勿念，受施慎勿忘。

4 **對朋友好，友誼到老；對敵人好，解怨結好。**
Do good to thy Friend to keep him, to thy enemy to gain him.

5 **想要被寵愛，得先能友愛。**
If you'd be belov'd, make yourself amiable.

6 **想要被疼愛，先去愛人，還得惹人愛。**
If you would be loved, love and be loveable.

7 **先愛人，就被愛。**
Love, and be loved.

8 保護神明，神也保庇你。

A noddo duw, ry noddir.

9 欠缺關懷的危害，大過無知造成的傷害。

Want of Care does us more Damage than Want of Knowledge.

10 大家都同意「寧可冒著失去朋友的危險，也不能少了笑料」是一件傻事。但是很少有人想過失去朋友有多麼容易：朋友間的丑角靠著朋友對自己的重視，才敢對朋友比對其他人放肆，而甚少考慮到我們所愛的人對我們的傷害會有多深。再怎麼緊密的交情，也沒辦法保障這樣的自由；而且仗著是朋友就能這麼做，實在是矛盾不通；除非我們能說，朋友對我們造成的傷害比其他人所造成的更小。

It is generally agreed to be Folly, to hazard the Loss of a Friend, rather than lose a Jest. But few consider how easily a Friend may be thus lost. Depending on the known Regard their Friends have for them, Jesters take more Freedom with

Friends than they would dare to do with others, little thinking how much deeper we are wounded by an Affront from one we love. But the strictest Intimacy can never warrant Freedoms of this Sort; and it is indeed preposterous to think they should; unless we can suppose Injuries are less Evils when they are done us by Friends, than when they come from other Hands.

11 送禮得當，能裂解「冰塊」。

Gifts burst rocks.

窮理查說：

「造訪當短，如冬日晝短，免得你太快就惹人厭煩。」

1 友誼靠著拜訪可增溫，但是不要常上門。
Friendship increases by visiting Friends, but by visiting seldom.

2 魚兒三日臭，訪客三日腥。
Fish & Visitors stink in 3 days.

3 女人、訪客、下雨天，只要三天，就會讓人打心裡生厭。

4 拜訪叔伯姑嬸，但是不要天天登門；探訪兄弟姊妹，但是不要夜夜見面。

Visit your Aunt, but not every Day; and call at your Brother's, but not every night.

窮理查說：

「惠而不費的事情別吝惜，好比禮貌、勸言和鼓勵。」

1 想受人稱讚，得先撒種子：說寬厚的言辭、做有用的事。
If you would reap Praise you must sow the Seeds. Gentle Words and useful Deeds.

2 啥都抱怨，或是啥都稱讚，都是鄉愿大蠢蛋。
Blame-all and Praise-all are two blockheads.

3 莫誇自家酒，莫讚自家馬，莫捧枕邊人。

4 若有人捧我，我也回捧他——把他當成最好的朋友那樣誇。

If any man flatters me, I'll flatter him again; tho' he were my best Friend.

5 酸言酸語，沒有朋友伴侶：一匙蜜糖引來的蒼蠅，多過一桶老醋沾上的螞蟻。

Tart Words make no Friends: a spoonful of honey will catch more flies than Gallon of Vinegar.

6 拍馬屁的人，一點也不蠢：被奉承的人，全部都當真。

A Flatterer never seems absurd: The Flatter'd always take his Word.

窮理查說：

「慷慨並不是給得多就贏，應該要給得夠聰明。」

1 援手給得適時，等於給了兩次。

Bis dat, qui cito dat.

2 最受期待的禮物，是回報而不是施捨。

Gifts much expected, are paid, not given.

3 過於有禮的脾氣，總是對自己無禮。

The too obliging Temper is evermore disobliging itself.

4 客套不是禮貌；禮貌不是客套。
Ceremony is not Civility; nor Civility Ceremony.

5 隨時彬彬有禮，其實做作到底。（編註：禮多必有詐）
Full of courtesie, full of craft.

6 感激千萬別過多，不然反而讓你找罪受。
Don't overload Gratitude; if you do, she'll kick.

7 誇讚要小，責備要少。
Praise little, dispraise less.

窮理查說：

「馬兒只想一件事，騎馬的人卻往往別有心思。」

1 評人莫只靠一點，要看他種種特質才完全。

Don't value a man for the Quality he is of, but for the Qualities he possesses.

2 人心隔肚皮，西瓜再甜也是隔層西瓜皮。

Men & Melons are hard to know.

3 小心在意回鍋肉，莫要輕忽宿敵來低頭。

4 人如果荒謬可笑，不是源自於他天生特質，而是他學來的習性才導致。

A man is never so ridiculous by those Qualities that are his own as by those that he affects to have.

5 小心脾氣來得慢的人：他們都有原因才動氣，而且不會沒事就消氣。

Beware of him that is slow to anger: He is angry for something, and will not be pleased for nothing.

6 最毒的蜜蜂從不說人壞話，不管是奴隸還是國王，但他的毒針最尖，而且扎下去絕不徬徨。

Speak with contempt of none, from slave to king, the meanest Bee hath, and will use, a sting.

7 隨聲附和者，千萬別信賴。

Approve not of him who commends all you say.

8 若有空穴來風往臉送，堅定意志，小心慎重。

If wind blows on you thro' a hole, Make your will and take care of your soul.

9 同一個人，不能既當朋友，又對你奉承。

The same man cannot be both Friend and Flatterer.

10 當心美酒所釀的醋，當心好好先生所發的怒。

Take heed of the Vinegar of sweet Wine, and the Anger of Good-nature.

11 真正的偉人既不會踐踏小蟲，也不會在帝王身邊偷偷摸摸。

大衛・巴里（美國普立茲獎得主）

《窮理查年鑑》帶給你很多笑聲，你甚至可能發現自己與窮理查的意見不謀而合，並且從中獲利。但我不得不告訴你，親愛的讀者，如果你只專注在文字形式上而忽略了內容的本質意義，你還不如乾脆把它們扔掉。

A true great Man will neither trample on a Worm, nor sneak to an Emperor.

（編註：Worm為雙關語，同時指小蟲和小人物，這裡指一個人不應欺侮不如己者，也不應奉承高於己者）

窮理查說：

「細察所有人──尤其是你自身。」

1 先把你手洗乾淨，再來指摘我汙點。
Clean your Finger, before you point at my Spots.

2 想摧毀你的敵人，自己就先做好人。
Wouldst thou confound thine Enemy, be good thy self.

3 知道自己屁股臭，就會特別在意別人皺鼻頭。
He that is conscious of a Stink in his Breeches, is jealous of every Wrinkle in another's Nose.

4 要批他人有過錯，捫心自問得先做。
E'er you remark another's Sin, Bid your own Conscience look within.

5 若要敵人不報復，管好自己是正途。
If you wou'd be reveng'd of your enemy, govern your self.

6 要愛你的仇敵，因為他們會指出你錯在哪裡。
Love your Enemies, for they tell you your Faults.

7 有種野心值得讚賞，就是要變得比鄰居更棒。
'Tis a laudable Ambition, that aims at being better than his Neighbours.

8 一旦失寵，沒人認識你；一朝獲寵，連你都不認得你自己。
When out of Favour, none know thee; when in, thou dost not know thyself.

9 對神明，必須敬畏又崇拜；對鄰居，必須公正又慈愛；對自己，要清醒又明白。

To God we owe fear and love; to our neighbours justice and charity; to our selves prudence and sobriety.

窮理查說：

「誘之以利，勝過說之以理。」

1 利益會使某些人看不到，卻讓其他人開竅。

Interest which blinds some People, enlightens others.

2 突如其來的權力，易成為無恥；突如其來的自由，容易變無禮；最好的辦法，是逐步給予。

Sudden Power is apt to be insolent, Sudden Liberty saucy; that behaves best which has grown gradually.

查理‧蒙格

我們還應該聽取隱含在富蘭克林所著的《窮理查年鑑》示諭裡的經驗教訓：「誘之以利，勝過說之以理。」這句睿智的格言，指出一個日常生活中偉大而簡單的道理：當你應該考慮動用「激勵」的力量時，永遠，永遠不要去考慮別的事情！

窮理查說：

「腐爛的蘋果會汙了周遭的蘋果。」

1 姑息壞胚子，結果反咬你一口；如果讓他吃苦頭，馬上乖得像條狗。

Anoint a villain and he'll stab you, stab him & he'l anoint you.

2 寬宥惡人，就是傷害善人。

Pardoning the Bad, is injuring the Good.

3 有時該睜開雙眼，有時該閉一隻眼。

There's a time to wink as well as to see.

4 只替好水果接枝，不然乾脆省一事。

Graft good Fruit all. Or graft not at all.

5 在腐敗的時代，為世界安排秩序反而會帶來混淆——管你自己就好。

In a corrupt Age, the putting the World in order would breed Confusion; then e'en mind your own Business.

窮理查說：

「把你受的傷害寫在沙子上，把你受的恩惠刻在大理石上。」

1 製造傷害讓你輸給敵人；報復他人只讓你跟他相等；只有原諒能讓你勝過他人。

Doing an Injury puts you below your Enemy; Revenging one makes you but even with him. Forgiving it sets you above him.

2 比起受傷就報仇，原諒顯得高貴得多，鄙夷更是有男子氣概得多。

'Tis more noble to forgive, and more manly to despise, than to revenge an Injury.

窮理查說：

「拿人說笑，樹敵不少。」

1 聰明往往反被聰明誤：玩笑並不總能被一笑置之，恍若無物。
Excess of Wit may oftentimes beguile: Jests are not always pardon'd—by a Smile.

2 笑話一出門，朋友帶進門，兩邊馬上吵一頓。
'Joke went out, and brought home his fellow, and they two began a quarrel.

part 4

窮理查教你健康、幸福過
好生活

仁慈的讀者：

受到您先前的慷慨所激勵，謹此向您呈獻本年曆……當您慷慨解囊，使我能添購家用必需，窮迪克也不忘要做些什麼來回報您的恩德。

我觀測星象就像是老貝絲監督著她女兒一樣，使您能早早知悉她們的一舉一動，而且還要細述她們的影響與效果，好讓您得到比夢見去年的積雪還要更多的好處。

無知的人會懷疑，我們星象學家能夠對天氣預測得如此準確，必定是跟古老的黑魔鬼訂下了交易。

欸！這簡直就跟尿床一樣簡單。

比方講，觀星者透過一只望遠鏡窺測天象……

他可能會看到金牛座，也就是那頭巨牛，在那陣狂奔之中，蹬著地板，甩動尾巴，伸長了脖子，咧開大嘴。從外觀上就很容易判斷出這頭憤怒的公牛在噴氣、喘息、咆哮。考量距離遠近，以及來到此處所需的時間，就能夠知道什麼時候刮風打雷。

他也可能看到了處女座（也就是那位少女）……她將頭轉向一邊，彷彿有人在窺視著她；微微彎著身子，手放在膝上，她若有所思地望向前方。星象學家能正確判斷出她在做什麼，經過計算了距離與所需時間，就會發現來年春天會有好一場四月雨。

還有什麼能比這更自然、更簡單的呢？我還可以列舉出許多其他例子，但是這已經足以證明我們不是魔法師了。

星象中蘊含了多麼奧妙的知識啊！即使是最細微的事項都載明在裡頭，只要你有技巧就能判讀。

當我的兄弟J-m-n想要知道到底是餵他那匹病馬一顆生雞蛋，還是餵點湯才對馬兒最好的時候，他發現星象明白指示要餵湯，所以他就讓馬兒喝了他的湯；現在，你認為那匹馬怎麼樣了？

你應該知道我接下來要說的了。

除了在年曆中常見的一般事項之外，我希望專業的人群導師能夠原諒我在書裡頭到處提供一些關於道德和宗教的訣竅。

而且，噢，莊重而清醒的讀者，如果在我書中有許多嚴肅的話語使你們覺得我絮絮叨叨、了無新意，也請你們不要覺得困擾。

我至今為您準備的餐點，都能保證物有所值。有些從智慧書上節錄來的話語，如果好好利用，可以為您的心靈提供豐富滋養。容易嘔吐的人吃飯不能沒有醬瓜；那沒有其他好處，但是至少能開胃。如果有虛浮的年輕人純粹為了笑話而讀我的年曆，或許會歷經到深刻的反省，使他終生受用無窮。

——《窮理查年鑑》一七三九年

許願求長壽，不如祈求好生活。

古人告訴了我們什麼是最好的；
但是我們必須從現代人身上發現
什麼才是最適合的。

窮理查說：

「吃得多，病痛多；藥不少，多沒效。」

1 健康萬分感覺不到，一點病痛就唉唉大叫。

We are not so sensible of the greatest Health as of the least Sickness.

2 一日三大餐，生活準完蛋。

Three good meals a day is bad living.

3 牙痛有帖藥方百試不誤：拿點老醋浸浸壞牙的根部，再給太陽晒半個鐘頭刻度──之後絕對不會再痛苦，保證算數。

An infallible Remedy for the Tooth-ach, viz Wash the Root of an aching Tooth, in

Elder Vinegar, and let it dry half an hour in the Sun: after which it will never ach more; Probatum est.

4 午餐吃得少，晚餐吃更少；要做得更好‥別吃晚餐就睡覺。

Dine with little, sup with less: Do better still; sleep supperless.

5 睡前沒吃飯，你就不會因為吃太飽而半夜起床。

Sleep without Supping, and you'll rise without owing for it.

6 晚餐吃得少，就不必吃藥。

Eat few Suppers, and you'll need few Medicines.

7 想要旅行四處跑，就該吃得少。

He that would travel much, should eat little.

8 起司、鹹豬肉，盡量要少碰。
Cheese and salt meat, should be sparingly eat.

9 熱的食物、辣的食物、甜的食物、冷的食物，全都容易傷牙齒，搞得牙齒像塊老豆腐。
Hot things, sharp things, sweet things, cold things All rot the teeth, and make them look like old things.

10 食物的量（非常可能）要與胃的性質和情況成比例，因為是靠胃來消化東西。
The Measure of Food ought to be (as much as possibly may be) exactly proportionable to the Quality and Condition of the Stomach, because the Stomach digests it.

11 吃是為了活，不要為了吃而活。
搞混了）

（編註：同時也比喻認清你真正的目標，不要和手段

12 飲食的適當質量一確定，就要能固定。正如飲食該恰到好處，其他事物也都別過度。

The exact Quantity and Quality being found out, is to be kept to constantly. Excess in all other Things whatever, as well as in Meat and Drink, is also to be avoided.

13 視個人體質攝取適量的飲食，參考指標是你的心靈做了多少事。書讀得多，消化就差得多，所以不該吃得像勞動多的人吃得那麼多。

Eat and drink such an exact Quantity as the Constitution of thy Body allows of, in reference to the Services of the Mind. They that study much, ought not to eat so much as those that work hard, their Digestion being not so good.

14 想活久一點，吃得少一點。

To lengthen thy Life, lessen thy Meals.

15 如果偶爾吃太多，省掉下一餐，應該就足夠，只要不是經常這樣做；例如如果午餐吃太多，晚餐、宵夜就跳過。

If a Man casually exceeds, let him fast the next Meal, and all may be well again, provided it be not too often done; as if he exceed at Dinner, let him refrain a Supper, &c.

16 不同體質，也該有不同飲食；同樣的東西對性寒的人可能太多，對性燥的人可能不夠。

And so do those of contrary Complexions; for that which is too much for a flegmatick Man, is not sufficient for a Cholerick.

17 簡樸的飲食可以讓人死亡的時候比較不痛苦，也可以讓各種感官充分發揮作用，也能緩和激情與情緒的波動。簡樸的飲食能夠維持記憶、增進理解、平息熱切的慾望，讓人思索他後續的目的，讓身體成為適合耶穌進駐的居所；而透過我們的救主耶穌基督，又能讓我們對現世感到滿意、對來世感到幸福。

A sober Diet makes a Man die without Pain; it maintains the Senses in Vigour; it mitigates the Violence of Passions and Affections. It preserves the Memory, it helps the Understanding, it allays the Heat of Lust; it brings a Man to a Consideration of his latter End. it makes the Body a fit Tabernacle for the Lord to dwell in: which makes us happy in this World, and eternally happy in the World to come, through Jesus Christ our Lord and Saviour.

18 要為了滿足必需來進食，不是為了口腹之慾而吃，因為慾望對於什麼叫必需，根本一無所知。

Eat for Necessity, not Pleasure, for Lust knows not where Necessity ends.

19 看病要及時：因為要是水腫過度，撐破皮膚，患者只能哀號著草藥沒效，這才去看醫生，才恨沒有及早。太晚受治療，財產有一半都花掉；一萬個醫生也沒辦法還他健康歡笑。

Watch the disease in time: For when, within The dropsy rages, and extends the skin, In vain for helebore the patient cries, And sees the doctor, but too late is wise: Too late for cure, he proffers half his wealth; Ten thousand doctors cannot give him health.

20

食物分量能足夠，就能把胃給填飽、讓胃消化好，滋養身體剛剛好。

That Quantity that is sufficient, the Stomach can perfectly concoct and digest, and it sufficeth the due Nourishment of the Body.

21

想要長壽、健康又明智，還要認識上帝所行的奇事？首先得讓你的胃口聽從理性的指示。

Wouldst thou enjoy a long Life, a healthy Body, and a vigorous Mind, and be acquainted also with the wonderful Works of God? labour in the first place to bring thy Appetite into Subjection to Reason.

22

如果吃到讀書、做事不舒服，那表示吃得太多。如果吃完覺得頭昏腦鈍，顯示吃了太多；飲食是要補給身體，使身心愉悅，不是要令人昏昏沉沉、身體遲鈍。如果覺得有這些不適症候，想想是不是吃得過度、喝得太多所導致，試著逐漸減少飲食分量，直到消除不適感為止。

If thou art dull and heavy after Meat, it's a sign thou hast exceeded the due Measure; for Meat and Drink ought to refresh the Body, and make it chearful, and not to dull and oppress it. If thou findest these ill Symptoms, consider whether too much Meat, or too much Drink occasions it, or both, and abate by little and little, till thou findest the Inconveniency removed.

23

適度的飲食可以避免疾病，這種方式可以令人少生病，如果偶然患病，可以比較承受得住，也比較快康復；因為大多數疾病的源頭都是暴飲暴食。

A temperate Diet frees from Diseases; such are seldom ill, but if they are surprised with Sickness, they bear it better, and recover sooner, for most Distempers have their Original from Repletion.

24

對抗疾病的最佳防禦，就是保護你的德性：節慾。

Against Diseases here, the strongest Fence, Is the defensive Virtue, Abstinence.

25

不想要冷天得到胸膜炎，不想要熱天患熱病和感冒──那就不要吃太多，別穿太暖和。

26

盡量避免看到美食佳餚；因為要在看到這些東西時覺得不開心，比避免沒看到卻想吃這些東西的慾望難得多了。

Keep out of the Sight of Feasts and Banquets as much as may be; for 'tis more difficult to refrain good Cheer, when it's present, than from the Desire of it when it is away.

27

年輕時、年老時、生病時，該有不同分量的飲食。

Youth, Age, and Sick require a different Quantity.

28

適度的飲食可以讓身體抵禦所有外在意外，讓身體不會受寒熱所苦，也不會因勞動而受傷；要是偶爾真的受傷、脫臼、瘀青，也可以比較容易治癒。

A temperate Diet arms the Body against all external Accidents; so that they are

29 難怪湯姆會肥胖，那個笨重的懶漢，他一生只吃了一餐──一頓永無休止的晚餐。

No wonder Tom grows fat, th' unwieldy Sinner, Makes his whole Life but one continual Dinner.

窮理查說：

「酒醉是眾惡之首，會讓某些人變傻子、某些人變野獸、某些人變惡魔。」

1 要說比傻勁，醉漢第一名。

Nothing more like a Fool, than a drunken Man.

2 把酒遞給聰明人，比他更聰明萬分。

Dyrro lynn y ddoeth e fydd ddoethach.

3 藉酒可以找靈感，最終還得靠水清醒定方案。

Take counsel in wine, but resolve afterwards in water.

4 藉酒澆愁愁更愁。

Drink does not drown Care, but waters it, and makes it grow faster.

5 酒後吐真言。

When the Wine enters, out goes the Truth.

6 把酒灑出來，只會損失那一點；把酒喝下去，往往連自己也搞不見。

He that spills the Rum, loses that only; He that drinks it, often loses both that and himself.

7 有人只顧飲酒，不管營生，每晚流連酒肆直到夜深，睡到日上三竿才起身，全家挨餓，何曾在意一分；上帝垂憐，拯救他這個人。可是啊，可憐了他老婆，倒楣萬分才會嫁他度過這一生。

He that for sake of Drink neglects his Trade, And spends each Night in Taverns till 'tis late, And rises when the Sun is four hours high. And ne'er regards his starving Family; God in his Mercy may do much to save him. But, woe to the poor Wife. whose Lot it is to have him.

8 可憐的迪克，吃起飯來像仕紳，喝起酒來像病人。

Poor Dick, eats like a well man, and drinks like a sick.

窮理查說：

「開會要趁用餐前；思考與行動，飽腹都覺得討厭。」

1 繆思女神愛早晨。
The Muses love the Morning.

2 肚子飽了，腦子就鈍了：繆思女神還在廚子那裡挨餓。
A full Belly makes a dull Brain: The Muses starve in a Cook's Shop.

窮理查說：

「路上有屍骸，老鷹就飛來，良法靠得住，人人遷來住。」

1 換床治不了感冒，換國家治不了當家的胡鬧。

Changing Countries or Beds, cures neither a bad Manager, nor a Fever.

2 正義一去，勇氣就虛。

Without justice, courage is weak.

3 只要鬧饑荒，法律沒人管；沒人管法律，饑荒馬上起。

Where there is Hunger, Law is not regarded; and where Law is not regarded, there will be Hunger.

4 太寬鬆的法律，很少人會遵行；太嚴苛的法令，很少能徹底執行。

Laws too gentle are seldom obeyed: too severe, seldom executed.

5 法網恢恢，像蜘蛛網只顧著抓蒼蠅，卻任憑大奸大惡溜過大眼睛。

Laws like to Cobwebs catch small Flies, Great ones break thro' before your eyes.

6 國王的起司有一半浪費在把皮給削掉；不過沒關係，削的都是民脂民膏。

The King's cheese is half wasted in parings: But no matter, 'tis made of the peoples milk.

7 糟糕的政府像河流，最輕的東西都漂在最上頭。

In Rivers & bad Governments, the lightest Things swim at top.

8 瘋狂的國王和瘋牛，再多的條約和繩索來綁都不夠。

Mad Kings and mad Bulls, are not to be held by treaties & packthread.

9 當官守法令，庶民聽官命。

The magistrate should obey the Laws, the People should obey the magistrate.

10 君子偉人，悲天憫人；懦夫暴君還不知道有事發生。

Great souls with gen'rous pity melt; which coward tyrants never felt.

11 沒有法律來維持，飯都沒得吃。

Where there's no Law, there's no Bread.

保羅·伏爾克（前美聯主席）

閱讀《窮理查年鑑》的樂趣在於品味他精闢的格言，作為床頭書也是很好的選擇，或是跟孩子介紹這一位美國的創始人，並提醒他們，有一些生活中的經驗和教訓是永遠不會改變的。

12 不管法官的判決帶來多少痛苦，但至少有一半人獲得彌補。

What pains our Justice takes his faults to hide. With half that pains sure he might cure 'em quite.

13 要是官員都不做好事，人民的善心就會餓死。

The Good-will of the Governed will be starv'd, if not fed by the good Deeds of the Governors.

14 給人官位沒問題，卻給不了他判斷力。

You may give a Man an Office, but you cannot give him Discretion.

15 設立太好的榜樣，是一種很少被原諒的毀謗──那是對權貴的中傷。

Setting too good an Example is a Kind of Slander seldom forgiven; 'tis Scandalum Magnatum.Setting too good an Example is a Kind of Slander seldom forgiven; 'tis Scandalum Magnatum.

窮理查說：

「別對你的醫生與律師亂說話。」

1 上帝時時行奇蹟——看哪！有一個誠實的律師在這裡！

God works wonders now & then; Behold! a Lawyer, an honest Man!

2 律師、牧師、山雀蛋，老是還沒長好就出頭。

Lawyers, Preachers, and Tomtits Eggs, there are more of them hatch'd than come to perfection.

3 窮困無律師。為什麼？因為沒有錢就沒律師。

Necessity has no Law; Why? Because 'tis not to be had without Money.

4 困境不顧法律；但我知道有好些律師就身處困境。

Necessity has no Law; I know some Attorneys of the name.

5 被控訴的可憐蟲要見律師面談，只能聲聲喚，因為律師聽不懂他的話，直到他付錢疏通。

Pillgarlic was in the Accusative Case, and bespoke a Lawyer in the Vocative, who could not understand him till he made use of the Dative.

6 夾在兩名律師中間的鄉下人，好比魚兒放在兩隻貓中間沒得翻身。

A countryman between 2 Lawyers, is like a fish between two cats.

7 底下三者無疑都是同一種人，牧師、律師和死神：死神帶走弱小的，也帶走強壯的人；律師不論是非，都照樣收費；牧師不管生死，都得拿錢才能要他辦事。

Certainlie these things agree, The Priest, the Lawyer, & Death all three: Death

takes both the weak and the strong. The lawyer takes from both right and wrong,
And the priest from living and dead has his Fee.

8 不要不舒服就看醫師，不要起口角就找律師，不要口一渴就找瓶子。

Don't go to the doctor with every distemper, nor to the lawyer with every quarrel, nor to the pot for every thirst.

9 吃藥多沒效，良醫最知道。

He's the best physician that knows the worthlessness of the most medicines.

10 好律師，壞鄰居。（編註：法不容情的律師難相處）

A good Lawyer a bed Neighbour.

窮理查說：

「愛之深，責之切。」

1 責備的尖刺，在於話裡顯真實。

The Sting of a Reproach, is the Truth of it.

2 嚴酷經常是仁慈；仁慈往往是嚴酷。

Severity is often Clemency; Clemency Severity.

窮理查說：

「婚前睜大眼，婚後半睜一隻眼、半閉一隻眼。」

1 想要良妻和良田，全靠丈夫自身賢。

Good wives and good plantations are made by good husbands.

2 只要有沒愛情的婚姻，就會有沒婚姻的愛情。

Where there's Marriage without Love, there will be Love without Marriage.

3 要駕馭馬兒，坐穩拉緊繩；要駕馭男人，鬆手且放任。

If you ride a Horse, sit close and tight, If you ride a Man, sit easy and light.

4 愛戀、咳嗽和香煙，都沒辦法藏著不讓人發現。
Love, Cough, & a Smoke, can't well be hid.

5 傑克若在談戀愛，就沒法對吉兒的美貌好好仲裁。
If Jack's in love, he's no judge of Jill's Beauty.

6 娶妻入戶，就有伴相護。
He that takes a wife, takes care.

7 想摘玫瑰總怕刺，想討漂亮老婆總怕戴上綠帽子。
You cannot pluck roses without fear of thorns, Nor enjoy a fair wife without danger of horns.

查理・蒙格

在《窮理查年鑑》中，富蘭克林提議：「婚前睜大眼，婚後半睜一隻眼、半閉一隻眼。」這種「睜一隻眼閉一隻眼」的方法，或許是正確的。

8 愛情與權力，最受不了別人來共享。
Love & lordship hate companions.

9 談戀愛的對象是自己，不會有情敵。
He that falls in love with himself, will have no Rivals.

10 沒有醜陋的愛情，也沒有美麗的監獄。
There are no ugly Loves, nor handsome Prisons.

11 你能忍受自己的差錯虧欠，為何不能忍受你妻子的缺點？
You can bear your own Faults, and why not a Fault in your Wife.

12 愛情和牙疼都有許多療方，但除了獲取和根除，沒有一個辦法屢試不爽。

Love and Tooth-ach have many Cures, but none infallible, except Possession and Dispossession.

13 快樂只是一陣風，功成事畢就不再吹送。（編註：十六世紀的諺語，指不要花太長的時間去追求一個人，速戰速決比較能幸福）

Happy's the Woing, that's not long a doing.

窮理查說：

「母親如果太勤奮，就會讓女兒變得又懶又鈍。」

1 偉人命雖好，可惜子孫傳不到。

The favour of the Great is no inheritance.

2 教子首先教修口，他很快就學會說話。

Teach your child to hold his tongue, he'l learn fast enough to speak.

3 美德，以及手藝，是小孩的最佳補品。

4 生前就將所有財產給兒子，一毛也不留：噢，蠢老頭！那好
比脫光身子才上床。

The old Man has given all to his Son: O fool! to undress thy self before thou art
going to bed.

窮理查說：

「不同教派就像不同的時鐘，內容差不多，彼此意見卻不同。」

1 許多人為了宗教爭吵，卻從來不曾按著行道。

Many have quarrel'd about Religion, that never practis'd it.

2 鐘聲會叫大家上教堂，卻從沒提醒佈道會那麼冗長。

The Bell calls others to Church, but itself never minds the Sermon.

3 有人自捫良心服神職，搜刮祭壇卻若無其事。

4
服侍上帝要靠與人為善，只是祈禱常被當成方便法門，所以才會吸引更多人。

Serving God is Doing Good to Man, but Praying is thought an easier Service, and therefore more generally chosen.

5
有多少人在慶祝耶穌的生辰！又有多少人遵行他的訓箴！噢！節日比教訓更容易留給後人。

How many observe Christ's Birth-day! How few, his Precepts! O! 'tis easier to keep Holidays than Commandments.

6
山姆的宗教就像切達起司，用的是從二十一個教區蒐集來的奶汁。

Some make Conscience of wearing a Hat in the Church, who make none of robbing the Altar.

Sam's Religion is like a Chedder Cheese , 'tis made of the milk of one & twenty Parishes.

7 獻神祭品搶不得。
Rob not for burnt offerings.

8 要靠信仰來看見，得先閉上理性之眼：吹熄蠟燭，才更覺得白晝光輝耀眼。
The Way to see by Faith, is to shut the Eye of Reason : The Morning Daylight appears plainer when ou put out your Candle.

15
WEALTH&
DREAM

15
WEALTH&
DREAM